To the memory of Mary Herrman—
strength from within.

ACKNOWLEDGMENTS

It was my good fortune to have the direction and encouragement of Ellen Schneid Coleman, my editor. She was the moving force each step of the way. Her constant support was invaluable.

Portions of this book were adapted from materials used in connection with seminars sponsored by National Seminars Group, a division of Rockhurst College Continuing Education Center, Inc. I am deeply grateful to them for their assistance and permission to use these materials.

My real recommendation for writing a book is to work with people who are incredibly creative, brilliant and fun and maintain it all even under the tightest time pressures. My heartfelt thanks to Carolyn Riddle and Deborah Shouse. Their lively illustrations and creative design give the perspective we hope the book conveys.

I owe sincere appreciation and admiration to the women in my seminars who share their stories of frustration, challenge and success as they continue to search for more effective ways to present themselves with impact, clarity and power.

And to my colleagues and friends, Recie Mobley, Sally Jenkins, Lisa Valenti, Susan Carnahan, Kay Keller, Sherri Cannon, Sharon Yoder and all the women on the faculty of National Seminars who gave me incredible support, spending hours of precious time sharing their workplace experiences.

Next, my thanks goes to JoAnne Linehart Thomas who meticulously read the entire manuscript, making sure every detail fit into the larger picture.

And finally to my husband, Jim, who was with me every step of the way. In addition to his emotional support, he lent his professional input and unique perspective.

INTRODUCTION

What you don't know can torpedo your career!

It's not just your education, training, and experience that get you ahead. It's speaking the language and knowing the unspoken rules.

What's the price if you ignore the rules? You'll be left out in the cold. The way people perceive you is more powerful than who you are. How you speak is more important than what you say. Clothes make a difference. Tears can keep you out of a corner office.

Like it or not, business culture reflects white male standards and behavior. Women are pressured and expected to conform to that norm.

While you may not want to talk like "one of the boys," or be a male clone, speaking a different language ensures you'll be misunderstood or not understood at all.

Women need to learn the "rules" of male-dominated business culture. They weren't taught the rules in business school. They've grown up in cultures where success is often measured by the ability to get along with others and be well-liked.

Women's communication style is typically passive, deferring and nurturing. Men's communication strategies, however, connote strength, power, assertiveness and security.

Successful career people are often competitive and ambitious, rather than cooperative and "nice." Expectations ingrained in children may conflict with skills needed in successful professional women.

In today's communication environment, you are caught in a paradox. You're expected to act as a woman and also as a professional. Employment occupies a major portion of our lives. You're obliged to work with professionals, yet you're reluctant to relinquish your feminine self-image in order to achieve.

During the 70s and 80s, women leaders emerged in the work force. In the 90s, women are no longer a token minority.

According to *Megatrends 2000* by John Naisbitt and Patricia Aburdene, women are becoming professional leaders:

- In the financial world, women have reached the halfway point.
- More than half of all officers, managers and professionals in the nation's 50 largest commercial banks are women.
- 49.6% of accountants are women.
- One-fourth of Wall Street's financial professionals are women.
- 30% of small businesses are owned by women.
- Women start new businesses at twice the rate of men.
- More than one-third of Procter & Gamble's marketing executives are women. 35% of Arthur Anderson & Company recruits are women. At the Gannett Company, Inc., almost 40% of the company's managers, professionals, technicians and sales force are women.
- Since 1972, the percentage of women physicians has doubled. Women lawyers and architects have quintupled.

♦ *Working Woman* magazine grew from a circulation of 450,000 in 1981 to 900,000 in 1988, surpassing *Forbes, Fortune* and *Business Week.**

WHAT THIS BOOK WILL DO FOR YOU

The 1990s is the most challenging decade the business community has ever confronted. In this book, you'll learn to develop techniques and practice your business communication skills through examples. You'll discover how to:

♦ Make your female strengths work for you.

♦ Recognize the stereotypical traps that can undermine credibility.

♦ Be assertive without being pushy.

♦ Manage your communication image.

♦ Deal authoritatively with difficult people and tough situations.

♦ Present yourself and your ideas with impact, clarity and power.

♦ Apply listening, one of the most powerful communication skills, to business situations.

♦ Use networking and mentoring to help you get ahead.

♦ Clear your career path of the most common obstacles to getting your point across.

♦ Successfully negotiate and influence others.

You'll also take the SELF Profile to gain personal understanding and self-empowerment techniques.

This is not a book about men and women in battle. Rather, this is a book about using confidence, assertive behavior and poise to get the recognition you deserve.

---

* Excerpted from *Megatrends 2000*. William Morrow & Co., Inc. by John Naisbitt & Patricia Aburdene. Copyright 1990.

DESIGNED FOR WOMEN WHO WORK

I've spent the last seven years speaking nationally and internationally helping women like yourselves gain the confidence, esteem and skills that make them stand out in their businesses.

Some of the comments I've heard from participants in training sessions include:

+ "Life is too short to put up with a bunch of nonsense. Your training builds confidence."

+ "Your seminar brought a new understanding to my job and to being a woman supervisor."

+ "Your course gave me much needed solutions to everyday problems in the office environment."

+ "We're excited about implementing the skills you taught and have greater confidence that we're on track. We left your training wanting more."

These women and hundreds of others inspired me to write this book.

I know how busy you are, so I've designed the book for a quick read. Every page has vital information you can take in at a glance. But reading isn't enough. You need practical information, "What do I do now?" It's in here: action you can take to make yourself into the business woman you want to be. Begin and end each chapter by taking an entertaining and informative quiz. Capture the essence of each chapter by making personal observations and notes.

This book gives you the confidence and business skills vital to your career. You'll work with your own innate abilities to become a more empowered business professional.

You deserve recognition and reward for all the hard work you do. This book gives you the know-how to ask for what you deserve.

TABLE OF CONTENTS

CHAPTER 8 PROVEN WAYS TO MAKE DECISIONS AND SOLVE PROBLEMS 157

CHAPTER 9 SUREFIRE WAYS TO FIRE UP YOUR PRESENTATION SKILLS 179

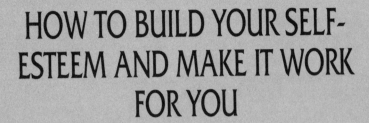

Chapter One

HOW TO BUILD YOUR SELF-ESTEEM AND MAKE IT WORK FOR YOU

SELF-ESTEEM: THE KEY TO HOW YOU COMMUNICATE

Rebecca has risen rapidly in her profession. She's one of those power women. She has won advertising awards for her creativity, her presentations and her graphic design work. She is smart, great at her work, a wonderful presenter, attractive and well-liked. Well-liked, that is, by everyone but herself.

"I wish I were better, I wish I were smarter, I wish I were prettier," says Rebecca. Her friend Marjorie looks at Rebecca, and wonders how she keeps up the facade. She wonders where Rebecca gets the energy to overcome her negative self-image.

SELF-ESTEEM IS HOW MUCH YOU LIKE AND APPROVE OF THE PERSON YOU
SEE YOURSELF TO BE.

Fast Fact

Self-esteem differs from self-confidence. Confidence blooms from a
feeling of esteem.

Action

Your self-esteem, how you see and envision yourself in the world, is vital to you as a woman in the work force.

When you increase your self-esteem, it positively affects:

+ How others treat you.
+ The choices you make.
+ The actions you take.

Self-esteem is the core factor in how you communicate.

Self-esteem comes from an inner acceptance and self-love.
When you have a comfortable level of esteem, you generate an exciting energy, a sense of aliveness and vitality that is irreplaceable.
With high self-esteem you acknowledge that you are the most important person in your world. As a woman you can have high self-esteem
without being egoistic or threatening. Your high esteem is a gift that
gets you noticed and appreciated in the business world. When you
have deep respect and unconditional acceptance of yourself, you
can have a genuinely high regard for others.

PROJECT YOUR MOST POWERFUL IMAGE

"Fall in love for fun and profit."

You'll profit from loving yourself, from the personal and professional empowerment you'll feel when you raise your self-esteem.
You'll be more visible, more attractive, appear more knowledgeable.
You'll be a more promotable woman. And you'll have a more balanced and pleasurable life.

You can better push through the glass ceiling and other invisi-
ble barriers created by a male-dominated power structure when you
view yourself as a person of great worth, enormous capabilities, and
unlimited talents. You need a sense of deep self-worth and glittering
self-esteem to overcome the fear of taking risks, asserting yourself,

pursuing your goals and dreams, developing your career and taking charge of your own advancement.

Test Your Self-Esteem

What sort of image do you project now? Are you *shining* with energy and power? Are you *shying* away from people and your own worth? Are you *scared* of proclaiming your needs? Take this test and find out.

1. It's the end of a hectic work day. You're meeting a potential client for dinner and you don't have time to go home and relax first. You have one hour before your dinner engagement. You:

    a. Stay at the office and clean up your desk. You don't want your boss to think you can't keep up.

    b. Go for a walk and, while you're briskly pacing, worry about all the work you have to do tomorrow.

    c. Leave the day behind. Enjoy a hassle-free drive to the restaurant. Take some deep breaths and clear your mind of today's concerns. Focus on the positive outcome with the potential client you are about to meet.

2. You have singlehandedly worked for three weeks, organizing a team building seminar. Although plenty of things go wrong at the last minute, the seminar is a huge success. Your boss invites you to the weekly director's meeting and tells the assemblage, "She handled the whole thing. She made it happen. I'm proud to have her in our company."

    Wow, your heart is WILD. You feel like doing a little tap dance right there. Instead you:

    a. Say, "Really, it was no big deal. Anybody could have done it."

    b. Look at a paper clip caught in the carpet and don't say a thing.

    c. Say, "Thank you. There were some long hours and I'm pleased to use my organizational skills to make such a great event happen."

3. Sally's husband is flying her to Rome for their anniversary. June's boyfriend is taking her to Greece. Just last Tuesday you made this wish: "I wish someone would pay to take me somewhere." Now you're in a board meeting and your supervisor says, "I have room for two more to go on this junket to Spain. I need senior staffers who haven't traveled yet this year." Your mouth is dry, your hands are moist. You fit the description perfectly. You:

   a. Clench your hands and stare at the legal pad in front of you. You don't really deserve such a great trip. You bite your lip and listen while others speak up.

   b. Your friend nudges you. "Speak up," she says. "No, really, I might hurt someone's feelings," you tell her. She nudges you again. "Speak up or I'll do it for you." You don't want to be embarrassed by her loud praise of you, so timidly, you raise your hand.

   c. You stand up and say, "I think I'd do a good job of representing the company on this trip. I meet the qualifications and I'd love to be part of this team."

4. You're not exactly excited about being the only woman invited to tour the newspaper plant. Your company is hoping to land the paper products for this huge account, so getting along with the other supporting vendors is important. Yet you notice the other vendors on the tour seem chummy with each other, like they're part of some secret society. The next time someone makes a remark that you don't get and everyone else laughs, you:

   a. Ignore it and look through your purse for an aspirin.

   b. Laugh along with them and act like you're having a wonderful time.

   c. Say, "It sounds like you all are enjoying something wonderful. I'd like to be a part of it."

5. Bev is smart, capable and attractive, one of your best workers. Yet she never takes credit for any of her accomplishments and seems to be stuck in her job. Whenever you recommend her for

a position change, someone always says, "She's too quiet. She can't handle people," and so forth. You believe in Bev and have a lot of confidence in her abilities. So you:

    a. Suggest she put in for some job that better uses her skills.

    b. Give Bev a highly visible project and hope she'll have the sense to take credit for it.

    c. Talk to Bev about how her shyness is getting in her way. Discuss some specifics and let her know you are willing to help her.

6. Of course, the manual should have been done yesterday, but many of the managers didn't get their articles in on time. You've worked most of the night and are struggling this morning to get the manual ready to print. It's good, but it could be better. Even though your manager told you meeting the deadline is more important than a perfect first-run, you aren't yet ready to let go of the document. You have one hour until deadline and you're exhausted beyond belief. You:

    a. Get a strong cup of coffee, eat a candy bar and read through the manual one more time.

    b. Give up. Figure, "If they wanted it right, they would have handed in their stuff on time."

    c. Ask someone you trust to do a quick proofread and editing job for you. Make sure they know your deadline. Know that you can't work a miracle in the last hour. Learn from this experience and have a plan of action to avoid the problem in the future.

SCORING

If you put down a lot of Cs, you are standing straight and *shining* out. Use this chapter to make your self-esteem even stronger.

If you drifted into Bs, you're the passive, deferring type. Speak up for yourself.

This is one test where straight As is not the ideal. It's hard to overcome the low self-esteem that so many women experience, but you can do it. Put the practical tips in this chapter to work for you and learn to appreciate and express your great qualities.

FAMILY MATTERS: HOW YOU GET YOUR SENSE OF ESTEEM

Patricia is the first person in her family to complete an advanced degree. She has two wonderful sons, a good job and is an expert quilter. Still, she looks at the ground when she walks and turns her head if you try to compliment her.

"None of the girls in our families feel good about themselves," Patricia says. "I think our Dad made us feel dumb when we were growing up. I guess it's just something I have to live with."

NO ONE NEEDS TO LIVE WITH LOW SELF-ESTEEM.

Fast Fact

You are not born with negative self-esteem. You learned it along the way. What you've learned, you can unlearn.

Action

Make a commitment to improve how you feel and think about yourself. Then have the patience with yourself you'd have with any dear friend. You're not going to be zapped with self-esteem overnight. The attitudes you took years to develop take time to undo.

From the moment one infant is wrapped in a blue blanket and another in a pink blanket, they are treated differently. As a woman, you are expected to think less of yourself, to undermine your credibility, to act passively and to put yourself down.

Perhaps, like Patricia, you suffer from low-esteem. Low self-esteem comes from the way the significant adults in your life treated you, especially during your formative years. Low self-esteem is not exclusively a woman's province, but men typically manifest their feelings of negative self-worth differently. Men often strip away their feelings of vulnerability and uncertainty and wear a brisk macho exterior.

Women, not wanting to waste a thing, wear their low-esteem. They drape it over their shoulders, perch it on their heads, wrap it around their waists. They show their feelings of doubt.

What causes the curse of low esteem?

- Lack of meaning or purpose.
- Little faith in yourself.
- Inability to accept responsibility for your well-being.
- Feeling dependent on others for approval or recognition.

♦ Not taking charge of your life; waiting for things to happen to you instead of making them happen.

While low self-esteem is painful, ask yourself, "What do I gain from my low self-esteem?"

♦ You can blame others— "It's because of my parents."
♦ You don't have to take charge.
♦ You have an excuse for staying in unhealthy relationships.
♦ You feel you don't need to change, because you don't deserve better.

High esteem leads to brilliant confidence. The woman who manifests this confidence enhances her powers of:

♦ Decision making.
♦ Problem solving.
♦ Knowing and expressing her rights.
♦ Managing her boundaries.

HOW TO ENHANCE YOUR SELF-ESTEEM

"It's not really my turn."
"No, I'm sure I'm not good enough to deserve this award."
"Oh my, I look terrible in this old dress."

WATCH OUT FOR NEGATIVE SELF-TALK THAT UNDERMINES YOUR SELF-ESTEEM

Fast Fact
Erase the old programming. Reprogram your internal message system with some positive affirming tapes.

Action
Self-esteem can be music to your ears. Get rid of that repetitive negative self-talk that says, "You're no good. You can't do anything right. You're not smart enough, pretty enough, brave enough, rich enough. . . ."

The Seven Step Self-Esteem-Building Exercise Program

1. **Stretch Your Mind and Get Rid of Negative Nagging**

    Much of this negative chatter is out of your awareness, but it affects you strongly. Take control. Act as though your mind is a reprogrammable computer.

    For 48 hours pay close attention to your self-talk. Keep a journal of your self-talk. The next time you make a mistake, stop and become aware of the thoughts or images that run through your mind.

    Notice:

    ◆ How much time did you spend being mad at yourself?
    ◆ What did you say to yourself? (Stupid, no excuse, ridiculous, and so forth)
    ◆ Did you forgive and accept yourself?

    When you do something right, notice the images that go through your head. Many women spend more time kicking themselves than they do congratulating themselves. How about you? When you do a great job, do you:

    ◆ Stop and praise yourself?
    ◆ Savor the feelings of self-worth you have?
    ◆ Listen carefully to the praise of others?

    The next time you daydream, be alert to what you are thinking about. Jot down these observations. You might be surprised at how harsh, critical and demanding your thoughts are.

    The good news is, you have a choice. With the next self-deprecating image you see, say STOP loudly so you can short circuit that undermining thought pattern. You have the power to erase and replace the negative barb with a positive thought.

    Your thoughts produce feelings which in turn produce behaviors. Strong positive thoughts translate into pleasant energetic feelings, which produce assertive strong behaviors.

2. **Your New Positive-thinking Workout**

    Work this out of your system:

    a. I don't have anything worth saying.

Work this in:

b. **I have a right to express my thoughts and be heard.**

Work this out of your system:

a. I am so stupid.

Work this in:

b. **I can learn whatever I need to learn. I'm as smart as anyone.**

Work this out of your system:

a. I can't believe I made a mistake.

Work this in:

b. **I made a mistake. I'm proud I took the risk.**

Work this out of your system:

a. I look terrible today.

Work this in:

b. **Maybe I'm not a Miss America runner-up today. So what. I'm clean, neat and smart.**

Work this out of your system:

a. I should be able to get more done in a day.

Work this in:

b. **I have a right to set my priorities and say "no" without feeling guilty.**

You know the routine now. Strengthening positive resolve takes a thousand repetitions. Replace each flaccid negative thought with a well-toned positive one.

3. **Flex Your Feelings and Fuel Up Your Esteem**
    The trade show has already started when Sandra arrives. Her job is to mingle, to get to know the other vendors. But Sandra's stomach is doing cartwheels. She hates crowds, she has nothing to say to anyone and she's worried she'll disgrace herself.
    "I'm scared," she whispers to herself.
    Her friend and co-worker Martha walks by. "How are you?" Martha asks.

"I'm scared," Sandra says.

"You look great. Go out there and fake it," Martha encourages.

Sandra takes a deep breath and begins to mingle.

WHEN YOU ACKNOWLEDGE YOUR FEELINGS, YOU STRENGTHEN YOUR SELF-ESTEEM.

Fast Fact

As a woman, one of your strengths lies in acknowledging and understanding feelings.

Action

Enhance your natural ability to feel your emotions and let them shape your esteem. By admitting your feelings, you own them, label them and can work with them.

Remember, just because you feel scared doesn't mean you are going to act scared. A basic law of success is: Act as though you are going to succeed. Assuming you will succeed is the beginning of making it possible.

For the kind of self-esteem that helps you shape a successful career:

- ♦ Notice what you are feeling.
- ♦ Acknowledge and validate your feelings, either to yourself by writing them down, or by telling a friend.
- ♦ Ask for any help you need pushing through the feeling.

---

4. Warm-ups and Cool-downs for a Positive Productive Day

Tina has already made breakfast for both her children and been successful in finding matching socks for them and un-run pantyhose for herself. She has 15 minutes to finish dressing, put on her make-up and dash off for work.

While she puts on her make-up, she talks to herself.

"I am so strong and brave," she says, spreading foundation on her face. "About that birthday card I didn't mail yesterday, it's OK. Don't sweat the small stuff. And don't worry about being peevish on the phone to that supplier. Those things happen."

She looks at herself as she brushes blush up her cheeks. "I am a good person. I deserve the best, the very best. I can take care of my needs." As she finishes her make-up and dressing, she repeats these last three sentences three times.

START YOUR DAY WITH A POSITIVE ZING AND A PROMISE OF GREATNESS.

Fast Fact

During your first and last waking moments, the subconscious mind is highly programmable. This is the golden hour of your day.

Action

Write four or five positive self-affirmations and repeat these ten times as the first and last thoughts of your day.

Try these to warm up and cool down your day:

1. I am what I am today and I'm becoming more each day.
2. My goals are important to me and I have the ability to achieve them.
3. I make healthy choices. I do not deny my needs or feelings to please others.
4. I accept myself unconditionally.
5. I learn from my mistakes and give myself the freedom to make them.

---

5. **Praise Builds New Muscles and Makes You Strong**

"Connie, that was an incredible presentation."

"Well, I could have done better if I'd had more time to prepare."

"Angela, the financial report was quite professionally done. Thank you."

"Really, it was nothing. Anyone could have done it."

"You look good today."

"This old dress has been in my closet for years."

MANY WOMEN FEEL COMPELLED TO POINT OUT A FLAW WHEN THEY ARE COMPLIMENTED.

Fast Fact

Women often think, "If I'm good at something, then it must not be important."

Action

The next time you are complimented, simply say, "Thank you." Nothing more. Bite your tongue if you have to. People with high self-esteem take credit for their strengths.

You may want to say, "Thank you. I like it too." or "Thank you, I appreciate your seeing me (it) that way." or "Thank you for noticing." or "Thank you. Your compliment means a lot to me."

As your self-esteem rises, you won't be so surprised by compliments. In fact, you'll give the compliment to yourself first, then hopefully, hear it a second time from somebody else.

---

6. **Get Into the "Positive" Shape That Makes a Difference**

Use your natural inclination to say positive things about other people as a strength. Often women are willing and adept at praising others.

When this is done from the heart, it builds your energy and puts you in an atmosphere that fosters self-esteem.

- Have tablets printed up with the heading, "I heard something nice about you today." Put them on everyone's desk and encourage people to jot down positive comments.

- Practice actively giving people positive feedback. Notice things you might otherwise take for granted.

7. **Pound Perfection Into Shape and Give Yourself a Break**

Don't keep yourself down by using perfection as your guidepost. Erase your "I have to be everything or I'm nothing at all" thinking and give yourself a delicious break.

Notice your attitude towards the mistakes of others. Are they foolish, reckless, stupid? Or are they simply a person trying their best who happened to make a mistake?

Now notice your self-attitude. Are you as kind and forgiving to yourself as you are to others? Do you have the same standards of excellence for yourself that you do for others? Or are you expecting to race up the corporate ladder carrying two children under one arm, managing the Miss America tiara on your head, a briefcase under the other arm, a frying pan attached on your right leg and a self-help library weighing down your left leg? And don't get slowed down by your mother who's clinging onto your back, or a spouse tugging at your skirt.

Think of the most rigid, demanding person you know. That's the face of perfection. Perfection allows no room for growth or mistakes. Perfection never forgives.

Excellence, however, gives you room to expand, take risks and make mistakes. Excellence rewards progress, learns from the past and builds toward the future. Excellence is loving and forgiving. Make it a point to give up perfection and strive for excellence. You'll give yourself freedom and space to grow.

SELF-ESTEEM: IT SPELLS SUCCESS

"Susan is so much better than I am. When I read her reports, it makes me not want to write," says Claire. "And have you seen the new suit Anna just got? It must have cost a fortune. I don't know how she does it. This old suit looks dumpy compared to hers. I'm trying to measure up to them, but I doubt I'll ever be that successful."

CREATE YOUR OWN DEFINITION OF SUCCESS.

Fast Fact
Constant comparison to others robs you of self-esteem.

Action
Ask yourself, "Whose definition of success am I using? My own or am I constantly feeling guilty or rotten because I don't measure up to someone else's definition of success?"

- Jot down four symbols of success per society. Many women write, "Money, power, status, clothes."
- Now write down your four symbols of personal success. These same women write, "Friends, health, marriage, children." Are you being driven by society's symbols of success? Are you striving for something that isn't even on your personal agenda?
- Focus daily on your definition of success. You are a winner if you achieve your own definition. Women have a tendency to give away personal power by feeling "less than" because they feel they don't measure up to society's definition of success.

What about your body image? Choose what you feel is a successful body image. Are you constantly feeling guilty because you don't look like the latest model on the cover of the latest women's magazine? Is that realistic? Do you really want to look like a magazine model or is a healthy, fit body your priority?

Society tries to foist an unreal ideal body on you. Resist, sisters! Don't spend another moment bemoaning your genetic make-up or your beautiful, natural aging process. The American culture makes it "good business" for women to focus on bodies and physical appearance as the cause of low self-esteem.

PATIENCE PLEASE. It takes time, patience and practice to uproot festering feelings of low-self esteem. Revise old negative images and replace them with glowing positive ones. And feel the glorious difference!

Remember, you have company on your journey to esteem. You may believe "I'm the only one who feels this way." Take comfort in knowing there are many who suffer from the drag and depression of low esteem. Talk to other women, join support groups or professional women's organizations. Being connected helps reduce the feeling of being overwhelmed by your own inadequacies.

Acknowledge Your Greatness: Let Your Esteem Shine

Take a new look at yourself. Notice your glow. Notice your increased strength. You're teaching people how to treat you and learning how to honor yourself. Take the quiz again and see if you've shoved away your shyness and are now shining brighter.

1. It's the end of a hectic work day. You're meeting a potential client for dinner and you don't have time to go home and relax first. You have one hour before your dinner engagement. You:

   a. Stay at the office and clean up your desk. You don't want your boss to think you can't keep up.

   b. Go for a walk, and while you're briskly pacing, worry about all the work you have to do tomorrow.

   c. Leave the day behind. Enjoy a hassle-free drive to the restaurant. Take some deep breaths and clear your mind of today's concerns. Focus on the positive outcome with the potential client you are about to meet.

2. You have singlehandedly worked for three weeks, organizing a team building seminar. Although plenty of things go wrong at the last minute, the seminar is a huge success. Your boss invites you to the weekly director's meeting and tells the assemblage, "She handled the whole thing. She made it happen. I'm proud to have her in our company."

   Wow, your heart is WILD. You feel like doing a little tap dance right there. Instead you:

   a. Say, "Really, it was no big deal. Anybody could have done it."

   b. Look at a paper clip caught in the carpet and don't say a thing.

   c. Say, "Thank you. There were some long hours and I'm pleased to use my organizational skills to make such a great event happen."

3. Sally's husband is flying her to Rome for their anniversary. June's boyfriend is taking her to Greece. Just last Tuesday you made this wish: "I wish someone would pay to take me somewhere." Now you're in a board meeting and your supervisor says, "I have room for two more to go on this junket to Spain. I ask that you be senior staffers who haven't traveled yet this year." Your mouth is dry, your hands are moist. You fit the description perfectly. You:

   a. Clench your hands and stare at the legal pad in front of you. You don't really deserve such a great trip. You bite your lip and listen while others speak up.

   b. Your friend nudges you. "Speak up," she says. "No, really, I might hurt someone's feelings," you tell her. She nudges you again. "Speak up or I'll do it for you." You don't want to be embarrassed by her loud praise of you, so timidly, you raise your hand.

   c. You stand up and say, "I think I'd do a good job of representing the company on this trip. I meet the qualifications and I'd love to be part of this team."

4. You're not exactly excited about being the only woman invited to tour the newspaper plant. Your company is hoping to land the paper products for this huge account, so getting along with

the other supporting vendors is important. Yet you notice the other vendors on the tour seem chummy with each other, like they're part of some secret society. The next time someone makes a remark that you don't get and everyone else laughs, you:

a. Ignore it and look through your purse for an aspirin.

b. Laugh along with them and act like you're having a wonderful time.

c. Say, "It sounds like you all are enjoying something wonderful. I'd like to be a part of it."

5. Bev is smart, capable and attractive, one of your best workers. Yet she never takes credit for any of her accomplishments and seems to be stuck in her job. Whenever you recommend her for a position change, someone always says, "She's too quiet. She can't handle people," and so forth. You believe in Bev and have a lot of confidence in her abilities. So you:

a. Suggest she put in for some job that better uses her skills.

b. Give Bev a highly visible project and hope she'll have the sense to take credit for it.

c. Talk to Bev about how her shyness is getting in her way. Discuss some specifics and let her know you are willing to help her.

6. Of course, the manual should have been done yesterday, but many of the managers didn't get their articles in on time. You've worked most of the night and are struggling this morning to get the manual ready to print. It's good, but it could be better. Even though your manager told you meeting the deadline is more important than a perfect first-run, you aren't yet ready to let go of the document. You have one hour until deadline and you're exhausted beyond belief. You:

a. Get a strong cup of coffee, eat a candy bar and read through the manual one more time.

b. Give up. Figure, "If they wanted it right, they would have handed in their stuff on time."

c. Ask someone you trust to do a quick proofread and editing job for you. Make sure they know your deadline. Know that you can't work a miracle in the last hour. Learn from this experience and have a plan of action to avoid the problem in the future.

GRAND TOTALS

You are ready to learn to love and accept yourself. You now know this is not a frivolous pursuit. This is a business decision on your part. Of course, it will also make your personal life much richer as well.

+ You are alert for negative self-talk.
+ You are replacing those old negative patterns with a positive affirming statement.
+ You know that it takes time and patience to build your esteem.
+ You're starting out your morning and ending your evening with affirmations, repeated at least ten times each.
+ You're learning how to accept compliments and how to give yourself compliments.
+ You're telling others how great they're doing.
+ You're overcoming your fear and acknowledging your feelings and you're asking for help and support.
+ What a relief! You no longer have to be perfect.
+ You're refocusing your energies around your own definition of success.

CAPTURING WHAT YOU'VE LEARNED

Things I've learned

_____

_____

Concepts I want to try

_____

_____

Great ideas I want to share with others

_____

_____

Things I want to know more about

_____

_____

Chapter Two

◇

MAXIMIZE YOUR STRENGTHS, MINIMIZE YOUR LIMITATIONS

Why worry about your SELF?

Your SELF explains who you are and how you relate to the people around you. With so many ways to interpret other people's behavior, why not take time to remove some of the guesswork. After you've taken the SELF profile, you'll understand more about your actions. You'll be more observant about co-workers' behavior and you'll learn to interpret the clues their behavior gives you.

SELF TEST

What behavior clues can you find in the following examples?

1. You say a warm "Good Morning." Susan rushes by with telephone messages in her hand, a pencil behind her ear, and barely acknowledges you. Why does she act this way?

   a. She's tired of your friendly tone and is snubbing you.

   b. She's afraid you're going to ask another favor.

   c. She's a self-determined, orderly woman, bent on getting a project completed by three o'clock this afternoon.

2. New Business on your agenda reads, "Plan marketing strategy for new product." So far your committee members have talked about their children and what sports they're playing. Why aren't they getting down to business?

   a. They're trying to impress you with their children's sports records.

   b. They're hoping you'll take over and do their work for them.

   c. They're gregarious and helpful workers frequently oriented to another person's issues. They are peacemakers and good listeners.

3. During the successful sales meeting, you bonded easily with clients, using your kind, caring personality. At the end of the meeting, Diane says, "Your expense account is three days late. And I need your monthly report tomorrow." Why does she behave that way?

   a. She's jealous of your glowing sales record and wishes it was hers.

   b. She thinks you're not paying enough attention to her.

   c. She has high departmental standards, and takes pride in being precise.

4. Stephan decides the office looks too cluttered with family snapshots, embroidery and posters on the walls. He orders his department returned to professional business-like status. Why does he make that demand?

   a. He thinks you're wasting too much time talking to Bridget, your sister-in-law, on the telephone.

   b. He needs you to think he's a dictator so you'll work harder.

   c. He's a practical, organized leader. Clutter frustrates him and makes him feel disoriented.

SCORING

If you answered As, you're about to unravel from carrying the world on your shoulders. Like many women, you internalize others' behavior and suspect people are trying to influence or manipulate you. You frequently wonder, "What do other people think of me?" The SELF Profile will give you confidence to rely on your own strengths and respect others' behavior for what it is.

If you answered Bs, you're engulfed in a world of hugs and slugs. Your strong nurturing skills are getting in the way of honest communication. The SELF Profile highlights your strengths and limitations. Learn how to take advantage of your nurturing skills and empower yourself with assertive communication skills.

If you answered Cs, you're well on your way to the top. You understand that each worker brings specific communication skills to the work setting. Use the SELF Profile to enhance clues you'll need to make it as an effective communicator.

Knowing your SELF takes the guesswork out of dealing with people.

Is Harvey being rude or is he an E in a hurry?

Is Angela totally unfocused or is she an L who wants to bond first?

Is Dana overly critical or is she an F who needs to get all the details straight?

And what about that maniac John? Is he totally unhinged or an S being expressive?

The SELF Profile gives you the answers.

THE SELF PROFILE

How much do you know about yourself? Are you constantly making lists and setting goals? Are you sensitive? When given a new assignment, do you plunge in to find answers or do you cautiously outline pros and cons?

Have you ever worked with someone who meticulously files

everything? When you relax, do you prefer parties with lots of people around or low lights and easy jazz?

Your behavior is affected by the situations you're in. Your social style is the result of many years of development. No personality style is better than any other. Yet you enhance your relationships with others if you understand your motivations, strengths and weaknesses, and those of people around you.

Each person has an environment she functions best in. Use the SELF Profile in this chapter to determine which of the four environments reflects your personality style. The SELF Profile is divided into four quadrants, or styles. Each style has characteristics. Although you're a unique blend of all four styles, one category will dominate. After you've taken this SELF Profile, you'll have a clearer understanding of how you interact with others.

The SELF Profile takes about 10 minutes. Use the scoring grid at the end of the inventory to better understand yourself and the people you work with. Use the grid to coach people you work with, or use it in conflict resolution. You'll feel more in control when you understand your strengths and weaknesses.

Self Profile*

The SELF Profile consists of 20 general questions describing how you might act in a given situation. Place the number that describes you best in front of each question. Answer with your first impression.

Not at all like me	Somewhat like me	Occasionally like me	Usually like me	Very much like me
1	2	3	4	5

_____ 1. When in a group, I tend to speak and act as the representative of that group.

_____ 2. I am seldom quiet when I am with other people.

* Excerpted from National Press Publications, Inc. *SELF PROFILE*, a division of National Seminars Group, © Copyright 1988, National Press Publications, Inc.

_____ 3. When faced with a leadership position, I tend to actively accept that role rather than diffusing it among others.

_____ 4. I would rather meet new people than read a good book.

_____ 5. Sometimes I ask more from my friends or family than they can accomplish.

_____ 6. I enjoy going out frequently.

_____ 7. It's important to me that people follow the advice that I give them.

_____ 8. I like to entertain guests.

_____ 9. When I am in charge of a situation, I am comfortable assigning others to specific tasks.

_____ 10. I often go out of my way to meet new people.

_____ 11. In social settings, I find myself asking more questions of others than they ask of me.

_____ 12. I truly enjoy mixing in a crowd.

_____ 13. Other people usually think of me as being energetic.

_____ 14. I make friends very easily.

_____ 15. I am a verbal person.

_____ 16. I try to be supportive of my friends, no matter what they do.

_____ 17. When I see that things aren't going smoothly in a group, I usually take the lead and try to bring some structure to the situation.

_____ 18. I seldom find it hard to really enjoy myself at a lively party.

_____ 19. When in a leadership position, I like to clearly define my role and let followers know what is expected.

_____ 20. I consider myself to be good at small talk.

_____ 21. I am very good at persuading others to see things my way.

_____ 22. I can usually let myself go and have fun with friends.

_____ 23. I often find myself playing the role of leader and taking charge of the situation.

_____ 24. I do not prefer the simple, quiet life.

For questions 25–30, please write in the letter representing your response at the end of each question.

25. You are in a conversation with more than one person. Someone makes a statement that you know is incorrect but you are sure the others didn't catch it. Do you let the others know?

   A. Yes

   B. No

26. After a hard day's work I prefer to:

   A. Get together with a few friends and do something else.

   B. Relax at home and either watch TV or read.

27. When planning a social outing with a small group, I am most likely to:

   A. Be the first to suggest some plans and try to get the others to make a decision quickly.

   B. Make sure everyone has a say in the planning and go along with what the group decides.

28. You have just finished a three-month project for which you have sacrificed a great deal of your free time and energy. To celebrate, are you more likely to:

   A. Invite some of your friends over and throw a party.

   B. Spend a quiet, peaceful weekend doing whatever you wish, either by yourself or with a special friend.

29. If I feel that I am underpaid for my work, I'm most likely to:

   A. Confront the boss and demand a raise.

   B. Do nothing and hope the situation improves.

30. I think that those around me see me as primarily:

   A. Gregarious and outgoing.

   B. Introspective and thoughtful.

Scoring Your SELF Profile

1. For items 25–30:
- ◆ If you answered A, give yourself a 5.
- ◆ If you answered B, give yourself a 1.

2. Now, transfer each of the scores you entered on the blanks below.

SAMPLE:

For example, if you answered "5" for questions 1–4, you would write your answers like this:

1. _____5_____   2. _____5_____

3. _____5_____   4. _____5_____

YOUR ANSWERS:

1. _____   2. _____

3. _____   4. _____

5. _____   6. _____

7. _____   8. _____

9. _____   10. _____

11. _____   12. _____

13. _____   14. _____

15. _____   16. _____

17. _____   18. _____

19. _____   20. _____

21. _____   22. _____

23. _____   24. _____

25. _____   26. _____

27. _____   28. _____

29. _____   30. _____

3. Add each column.

DIRECTIVE SCORE _____   **AFFILIATIVE SCORE** _____

If you scored from: Give yourself a:

If you scored from:	Give yourself a:
15–21	1
22–33	2
34–44	3
45–56	4
57–68	5
69–75	6

4. Using the chart on the facing page, take your **Directive Score** and put a dot on the broken line. This line shows your needs and tendencies to direct and control situations. People scoring high on this line are comfortable supervising others and controlling situations. People scoring low on this line are generally more supportive and seek consensus from others.

5. Now, put a dot on the dotted line for your **Affiliative Score.** The Affiliative line measures your needs and desires for being around others. If you scored high on the line, you probably like it best when you're with people. If you scored low, you tend to be more self-contained, enjoy time to yourself or with a few close friends and generally seek less interaction with others.

6. Connect the two dots with a straight line.

7. Shade in the area between the line you've drawn and the intersection of the broken and dotted lines. The category you've shaded in reveals where you feel psychologically safe most of the time, and especially when you're under stress. We all reveal some characteristics in all categories. But the shaded category is your most comfortable zone.

8. Review the SELF social dimensions. Which dimension are you most likely to get along with?_____

_____

9. List three of your colleagues and decide which dimension they might fit into. _____

_____

Figure 2–1

Follow the directions in 4–7 and plot your SELF characteristics.

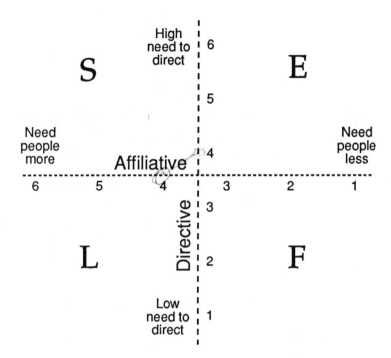

10. What social tendencies do you have that could jeopardize you in interacting with any of the other dimensions? _____

_____

_____

11. Review the SELF social dimensions. Which dimensions are you most likely to get along with? Where are you most likely to experience problems? _____

_____

12. People are motivated for their own reasons. What motivates you? _____

_____

_____

Figure 2–2 (a)

Notice the characteristics that describe the tendencies of each dimension of the SELF.

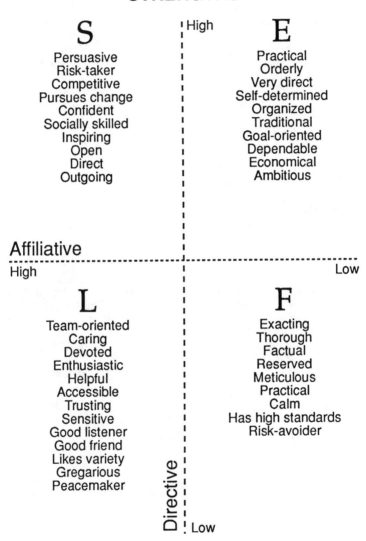

STRENGTHS

S — High — **E**

S	E
Persuasive	Practical
Risk-taker	Orderly
Competitive	Very direct
Pursues change	Self-determined
Confident	Organized
Socially skilled	Traditional
Inspiring	Goal-oriented
Open	Dependable
Direct	Economical
Outgoing	Ambitious

Affiliative

High — Low

L — **F**

L	F
Team-oriented	Exacting
Caring	Thorough
Devoted	Factual
Enthusiastic	Reserved
Helpful	Meticulous
Accessible	Practical
Trusting	Calm
Sensitive	Has high standards
Good listener	Risk-avoider
Good friend	
Likes variety	
Gregarious	
Peacemaker	

Directive — Low

Continued

Figure 2–2 (b) *(cont'd)*

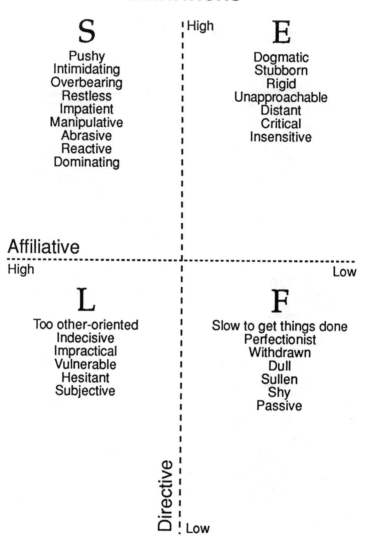

LIMITATIONS

S	E
Pushy	Dogmatic
Intimidating	Stubborn
Overbearing	Rigid
Restless	Unapproachable
Impatient	Distant
Manipulative	Critical
Abrasive	Insensitive
Reactive	
Dominating	

High

Affiliative
High   Low

L	F
Too other-oriented	Slow to get things done
Indecisive	Perfectionist
Impractical	Withdrawn
Vulnerable	Dull
Hesitant	Sullen
Subjective	Shy
	Passive

Directive
Low

Figure 2–3 (a)

What turns you on? Off? Examine the turn-ons and turn-offs for people with whom you work.

TURN-ONS

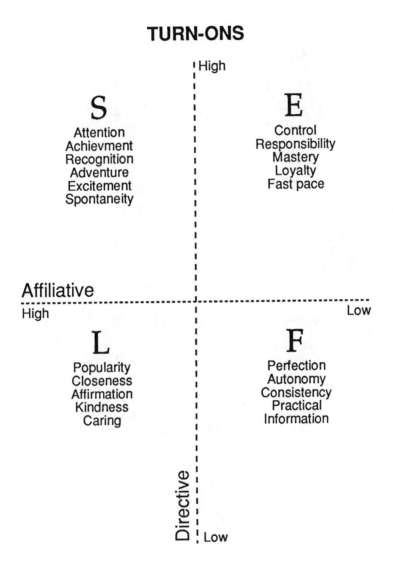

Continued

Figure 2–3 (b) (*cont'd*)

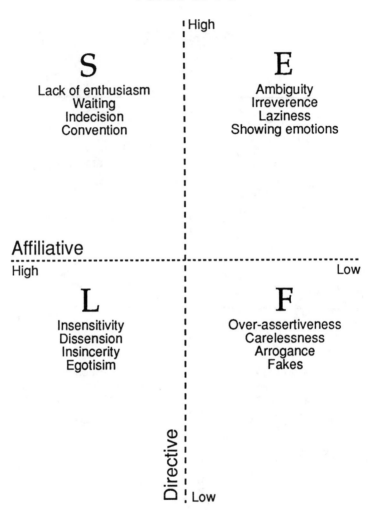

TURN-OFFS

High

S
Lack of enthusiasm
Waiting
Indecision
Convention

E
Ambiguity
Irreverence
Laziness
Showing emotions

Affiliative
High   Low

L
Insensitivity
Dissension
Insincerity
Egotisim

F
Over-assertiveness
Carelessness
Arrogance
Fakes

Directive

Low

Figure 2–4

Personalities on the right side only and on the left side only are similar and are most likely to get along in a work setting. Ss and Ls are most compatible, as are Es and Fs.

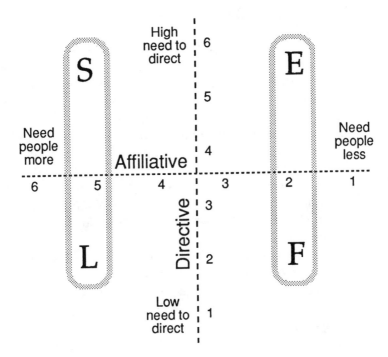

FINDING YOUR SELF

The *S* Personality

Sharon is an excellent telemarketer who doesn't seem to know a stranger. She can put a smile on anyone's face since she almost always appears to be in a great mood.

Most of the time she's articulate and entertaining when she speaks. She can sell anything, loves to party, and answers direct questions with a direct answer. When the group talks about going out for lunch, she's the first one at the door, inspiring others to come along. If the party gets dull, she'll come up with a new activity.

She dresses in flamboyant prints, stripes and polka dots. Her office appears to be extremely disorganized, yet if you ask her for the Phoenix file, she knows exactly where it is.

Count on Sharon to be confident, competitive and creative. When she finishes a big project, she seeks recognition such as a cash bonus, a raise, or a new job title. She might consider a fancy office or socially-oriented benefits in lieu of cash.

Sometimes people think she's intimidating and overbearing. When the committee doesn't see things her way, her persuasive skills come alive. She may appear manipulative or dominating.

The *E* Personality

Laura doesn't need peer recognition. Each morning, she reads the *Wall Street Journal* and writes a fresh list of daily goals. She balances her checkbook after writing each check. She puts 30 percent of each paycheck into mutual funds, she invests in real estate and spends less than 2 percent of her check on entertainment.

Laura has practical and ambitious ideas. She can be depended upon to carry out every idea she recommends. When it's time to assign tasks, she's not worried about other workers' feelings getting in the way. She blocks out things she doesn't want to hear because her main concern is to get the job done.

When she reviews a proposal, Laura flips through the pages, searching for the bottom line. She wants an executive summary, a financial report, and a flow chart. If she needs more, she'll tell you.

Laura feels little need to get close to people. Now and then, she'll show up at a party, but if she can't discuss how to run a department or organize the food table, she'll find an excuse to leave early.

Her co-workers say, "Laura doesn't get ulcers. She gives them." She appears stubborn, rigid, critical and insensitive. But Laura feels she has to be this way to be dependable.

The *L* Personality

An administrator in the real estate industry, Roberta runs her office with an open-door policy. People enter her office because they know she'll listen to their problems and she'll show enthusiasm for their projects.

When there's a disagreement between co-workers, one or both workers will end up talking out issues with Roberta. She keeps hot chocolate, tissues, hand lotion and aspirin in her desk just for those moments.

Roberta's office reflects her gregarious, accessible nature. She has plants in three corners, pictures all over the walls, a coffee pot and extra mugs.

When she first joined the company's management, she worked diligently to create an open, friendly environment.

Sometimes Roberta feels like she pours too much of herself into other people's problems. She can make decisions for other people, but is indecisive about her own issues. When managing a project, she might keep a tight handle on spending, or she may be impractical with her budget.

When she's most frustrated, she wishes someone would return the listening favor.

The *F* Personality

Eleanor is a practical, calm dental specialist with a national health care corporation. She remembers details from last year's cases and sets high standards for herself and her co-workers. Her department manager depends on Eleanor to find every undotted "i" and uncrossed "t."

Eleanor loved her old office tucked away in the back of the 13th floor. No one asked her to "hurry up," no one peeked into her office just to say "hi." If she didn't want the telephone to interrupt her concentration, she let her voice mail pick up her messages.

But when the company reconfigured, they moved Eleanor's office into a cluster with underwriters and medical sales reps so that she could be a resource for them. Now she dislikes going to work. She's expected to give "instant" answers. The telephone rings constantly. She is absolutely convinced that accuracy will make or break the health care industry and if anyone wants an answer from her, she must have time to investigate.

Her office is loaded with file cabinets, textbooks, slides and charts. She has one picture on the wall, which she straightens every morning.

Eleanor just wants to go back into the corner where she can mind her own business, do her job, and get it done right.

PUTTING THE SELFS TOGETHER

Suppose you're the corporate executive who wants to set up a "Feed The Homeless" fundraiser for your company. Last year your competition scheduled the fundraiser, got plenty of publicity, a key to the city, and a dinner invitation from the Mayor.

You set up committees to plan the fundraiser and place each committee in a separate room. Each committee is made up of four people who are high in each profile. One hour later, you return to see what ideas they've come up with. Soon, you realize the importance of mixing people from each SELF social dimension.

THE FOUR HIGH Ss: They haven't accomplished a thing, but they had a great time together. The table is littered with popcorn and empty cola cans. One person has turned the pencils and paper into a rhythm and blues band. Paper is scattered across the table, and they're in the middle of their 20th joke when you enter the room.

THE FOUR HIGH Es: They also accomplished very little. Two pencils are untouched, still neatly placed in the center of the table, otherwise the table is bare. They sit straight, the air feels like an IRS audit while each struggles for dominance.

THE FOUR HIGH Ls: The table is covered with family photos and an empty Whoppers box. The telephone is still warm. They're not really clear about what they're supposed to do, but they'd like to start by taking a collection for the homeless.

THE FOUR HIGH Fs: At first, they don't acknowledge you, until one person says she needs more time. They look exhausted, and reams of paper cover the table to show their progress. They would have formed committees with lengthy agendas for follow up if you'd only given them a few more minutes.

Broadening the Dimensions: Your Key to Getting Along in a Group

Twila decided to bring one person who scores high, unwilling to flex, from each dimension into her committee. As an S, she's a risk-taker, and confident she can pull off the fundraising event. Especially if she assigns specific tasks to each committee member.

During the meeting, Edwin, an E, sits with his arms crossed, his voice gets louder with each idea he presents. Larry, an L, passes out gum to each committee member, while Frances, an F, holds her hands over her ears.

When Edwin slams his hands on the table, complaining that no one is listening to his ideas, Twila says, "Who died and left you the boss?"

TO GET ALONG IN A GROUP, YOU MUST FLEX YOUR SOCIAL DIMENSIONS.

Fast Fact
Perception is reality. The way you see the world is the way you *think* things are.

Action
Just because your style works for you doesn't mean it works for everyone else. People are not difficult, but they may appear difficult because their communication styles are different.

- Encourage people to work together by understanding the strengths of each social dimension.
- Surround yourself with people who have social skills different from yours. Each person grows up using language in a different way. Use these differences to make a well-functioning team.
- Flex your own social dimensions. The closer you scored to the center of the grid, the easier it is for you to flex in and out of other dimensions.
- Respect your own profile and social differences. Review the turn-ons and turn-offs grid. What do you need for psychological safety?

_____

_____

- How can you make the most of your strengths and still rely upon others?

_____

_____

- Be willing to accept gender differences. Do you know what they are?

MALE AND FEMALE REALITIES

Your "reality" is how you interpret things that happen to you and how you make adjustments. But just how did you get to be? What are some of the differences between male and female communication?

The Reality Check

Use the following code for each of these statements:

a = *usually applies to women*   **b** = *usually applies to men*

_____   1. Takes a greater interest in relationships, sharing, cooperation, intuition.

_____   2. Interested in results, achieving goals, power, competition, work, logic, efficiency.

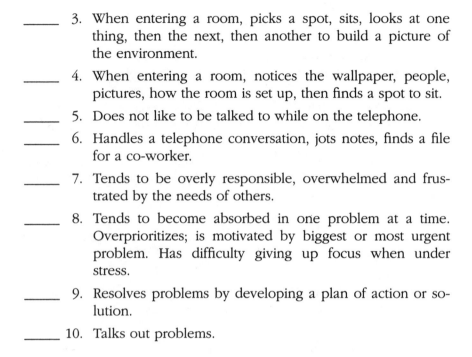

_____ 3. When entering a room, picks a spot, sits, looks at one thing, then the next, then another to build a picture of the environment.

_____ 4. When entering a room, notices the wallpaper, people, pictures, how the room is set up, then finds a spot to sit.

_____ 5. Does not like to be talked to while on the telephone.

_____ 6. Handles a telephone conversation, jots notes, finds a file for a co-worker.

_____ 7. Tends to be overly responsible, overwhelmed and frustrated by the needs of others.

_____ 8. Tends to become absorbed in one problem at a time. Overprioritizes; is motivated by biggest or most urgent problem. Has difficulty giving up focus when under stress.

_____ 9. Resolves problems by developing a plan of action or solution.

_____ 10. Talks out problems.

Answers:

1. a   2. b   3. b   4. a   5. b   6. a   7. a   8. b   9. b   10. a

SCORING

9–10 correct: Congratulations, you are aware of basic gender differences.

7–9 correct: Sometimes you're confused by the fundamental differences between men and women. You're not alone! Keep reading and ease some of your frustrations.

4–6 correct: You need to rediscover a powerful strength: the intuition necessary to respect each gender's unique qualities. Take heart. You're not the one from Mars.

Satellite Dish vs. The Bull's Eye

When she arrives at the company's 75th Anniversary Celebration, Jantele glances around the lobby, wondering where to begin. While she checks her coat, she notices two friends standing beside a bronze statue, red bows tied to the marble pillars, the band members' sleek tuxedos, and a table of hors d'oeuvres. Once inside, she stops at the food table, then finds a place next to her friends.

James arrives right behind Jantele. He stands at the door for a moment, checks his coat, then finds a place to sit next to his boss. Once seated, he looks at the band and analyzes their instruments, their sound system, their age. Then, he looks to the group of women talking near the stage. Gradually, he builds a picture of his environment.

MEN AND WOMEN VIEW THEIR ENVIRONMENTS FROM DIFFERENT PERSPECTIVES.

Fast Fact

While men view the world from a focused, sequential perspective, women see the whole picture at once. Both views are valid.

Action

Women are like satellite dishes taking in 130 channels at once. Men are like the bull's eye on a dart board. Both receive information, both have a unique value in the workplace. Subtle linguistic differences create barriers to open, healthy communication.

Women look for stereotypical things that make them feel comfortable. This helps them get grounded as it affirms their identities. When using the powerful communication skills discussed, you'll gain confidence in self-expression.

If you want a man to focus on your conversation, and you can see his attention is already focused elsewhere, ask, "When would be a good time to talk?"

If he says, "We can talk now," but doesn't stop what he's doing, don't be fooled. He is unaware of the limits he's placing on you. Men, especially when under stress, have difficulty releasing their focus. Rather than resent him for not listening, you can:

+ Wait quietly until he looks at you.
+ Tell him you really need his full attention.
+ Put your request in writing and set up a time to discuss your topic.
+ The morning of the meeting, give him a reminder.

ESTABLISH YOUR MOST POWERFUL COMMUNICATION ENVIRONMENT

Judith is the administrative assistant at a major publishing house. Her desk is unorganized. Her files are out of date. She finds it difficult to keep her mind on a single project. She seldom meets deadlines. By Friday she's a nervous wreck. She dosen't understand why David, her boss, never seems to listen to her and says she's had it with his action plans. She wishes she could pack her sporty car and move to some exciting city.

PUT THE RIGHT PEOPLE WITH THE RIGHT JOB.

Fast Fact
Your job placement has a direct effect on your level of success.

Action
Use what you learned from the SELF Profile and "Gender Realities" to know yourself.

+ What do you do well?
+ What's the best use of your talents, your creativity?
+ What are your strengths? Your soft spots?
+ How do you rely upon others? When did you do this last? How did you feel?

Knowing your SELF helps you:

+ Maximize your strengths.
+ Work effectively with your team by valuing, respecting, and utilizing diversity.
+ Set the scene for effective communication.
+ Ask for and receive your optimum communication environment.

Spot the Different Selfs in Your Workplace

How quickly can you spot the different SELFs? Who do they remind you of in your workplace?

1. You say a warm "Good Morning." Susan rushes by with telephone messages in her hand, a pencil behind her ear, and barely acknowledges you. Why does she act this way?

   a. She's tired of your friendly tone and is snubbing you.

   b. She's afraid you're going to ask another favor.

   c. She's a self-determined, orderly woman, bent on getting a project completed by three o'clock this afternoon.

2. New Business on your agenda reads, "Plan marketing strategy for new product." So far your committee members have talked about their children and what sports they're playing. Why aren't they getting down to business?

   a. They're trying to impress you with their children's sports records.

   b. They're hoping you'll take over and do their work for them.

   c. They're gregarious and helpful workers frequently oriented to another person's issues. They are peacemakers and good listeners.

3. During the successful sales meeting, you bonded easily with clients, using your kind, caring personality. At the end of the meeting, Diane says, "Your expense account is three days late. And I need your monthly report tomorrow." Why does she behave that way?

   a. She's jealous of your glowing sales record and wishes it was hers.

   b. She thinks you're not paying enough attention to her.

   c. She has high departmental standards, and takes pride in being precise.

4. Stephan decides the office looks too cluttered with family snapshots, embroidery and posters on the walls. He orders his department returned to professional business-like status. Why does he make that demand?

   a. He thinks you're wasting too much time talking to Bridget, your sister-in-law, on the telephone.

   b. He needs you to think he's a dictator so you'll work harder.

   c. He's a practical, organized leader. Clutter frustrates him and makes him feel disoriented.

GRAND TOTALS

In this chapter, we reviewed some essential keys to learning about your SELF. Using the SELF in the workplace, you'll be more observant about co-workers' behavior and understand what their behavior is telling you. Here are some things covered in this chapter:

+ Every successful group needs people from each dimension.
+ Co-workers who are flexible create the best working teams.
+ You function best in an environment that suits your SELF profile.
+ Communication works well when you understand the strengths of each dimension.
+ You have a clearer definition of your communication style.

CAPTURING WHAT YOU'VE LEARNED

Things I've learned

_____

_____

Concepts I want to try

_____

_____

Great ideas I want to share with others

_____

_____

Things I want to know more about

_____

_____

Chapter Three

◇

PRESENT A POWERFUL, POSITIVE IMAGE
How to Project Your "Star" Qualities

Watch out! You have seven seconds to make a first impression. This is your initial screen test. How do you project yourself?

SCREEN TEST

1. You are in a meeting. You've made a suggestion and your boss turns away from you, looks at Bill and says, "I'd like to hear something important from you." How do you respond?

   a. "Gary, before we move on, I want to know what part of my message you think is not important." You look directly at your boss, lean forward and use a firm tone of voice.

b. You push your chair away, sigh and mentally escape.

c. You chuckle and agree with your boss. "Yeah, my ideas are usually off-the-wall. Can I get you some coffee?"

d. "Excuse me, Gary," you say. "What I said was important. Don't put me down in front of this group."

2. Joe comes into your office, yells profanity at you in front of others because of a missing report. What do you do?

   a. Hold your ground. Stand up, cross your arms and lean slightly forward and say, "Let's talk about the missing report."

   b. Deny that Joe is in your office. Look away. Pretend he's not there.

   c. Profusely apologize for the missing report.

   d. Scream back at Joe.

3. You have recently been promoted from the ranks. Linda, who has more seniority than you, resents your promotion, and is being uncooperative at every step. How do you react?

   a. "Linda, as your supervisor, you can expect fairness and co-operation from me and I expect the same from you. I want to talk about how we can both get our needs met."

   b. Avoid contact with Linda. Take the stairs if she's in the elevator. Exclude her from meetings as well as casual conversation.

   c. "Linda, I feel so guilty that you didn't get the promotion. Everyone knows you have more seniority. I don't understand why they did this."

   d. "Linda, I know you resent my promotion and your present attitude should prove why you didn't get the job."

4. You're a manager in a small company that's on the move. The CFO recently gave you an exceptionally high performance rating, so you're expecting a raise. When you discuss this with him, you're told "the company profit margin is down. You'll have to wait five months." How do you respond?

   a. "I appreciate the company's financial situation at this time. I believe my evaluation proved that I am valuable to the company. In five months, I'd like to talk about making the salary increase retroactive."

   b. "I'm so sorry to hear about your poor profit margin. Do you think in a few months we'll be able to discuss my salary increase?"

   c. "You are right. How insensitive of me. Don't give it another thought."

   d. "You're not being fair! I wouldn't have worked so hard if I thought you weren't going to give me a raise."

5. At a working lunch meeting of male colleagues, you are the only female supervisor. You are asked to take notes and keep a fresh pot of coffee brewing. What do you say?

   a. "I would prefer someone else take notes and I made coffee at our last meeting. I need to devote my full attention to this meeting."

   b. "I'd be happy to act as secretary. Actually, I should have started coffee earlier this morning."

   c. "Excuse me. I'm not feeling very well. I don't think I should stay for this meeting."

   d. "You're all a bunch of male sexists. I resent your macho implication that women do your menial tasks."

6. You're the project coordinator on a huge sales presentation, but you're doing all the work. Jackie, a co-worker, has shown your slides and printed material to your boss and is taking credit for the material. What do you do?

   a. "Both of our names are listed on this project description, yet I'm doing all the work. I'd like to talk to you about sharing the work and the credit."

   b. You remain silent. Cream rises to the top, you tell yourself, and quietly resent your boss's lack of appreciation.

   c. You decide if Jackie wants all the credit, she can have it. You resign from the project and hope your boss will discover who is the real worker.

d. "You're ignoring this project, yet you're willing to take credit for my work. I'm telling the boss."

7. You inherited a budget that doesn't match your goals, so you're carefully managing your department's consumables. Tony, manager of computer design, is planning a corporate event and requests materials from you. What do you say?

a. "I'm having trouble meeting my budget, Tony. I prefer to not make extra materials available unless it's essential. Tell me about the event and we'll explore some solutions."

b. "I'm sorry, but I'm out of the materials you need. I might be able to help you next week. Is that okay?"

c. "I have no budget to provide these materials for you. I don't make the rules."

d. "You shouldn't ask for more materials! I'm over budget myself. I can't give you anything."

8. Emily, your employee, isn't working up to the goals she agreed upon. When reviewing her performance, you say:

a. "We agreed on certain goals and I've noticed you're having trouble achieving them. Let's discuss the choices available in order to improve your performance."

b. "It's obvious the goals we set are too much for you. I'm going to find a job for you that fits your limited abilities."

c. "You know the rough part of my job is, well, I just don't want to hurt your feelings. Do you think we could have a friendly chat about your work?"

d. "You're a sloppy worker. I don't think you care about this job."

SCORING

How did you feel about some of the answers? Did you feel some answers made you a winner or loser?

If you chose all As, then you selected situations where everyone wins. Bs? Both parties end up losers. If you selected a C, then you sacrificed your needs for the sake of others. You lost, they won. If you selected any Ds, you won, but the other person lost.

You deserve a starring role in your organization. That's what this chapter is about: how to project the confident, strong image that gets you ahead.

YOUR SCRIPT: HOW TO AVOID SPEECH PATTERNS THAT MAKE YOU SEEM LIKE A LIGHTWEIGHT

Regina collates indexing tabs and design layouts from several tables as she assembles notebooks. People in her department have been scrambling for hours to help her meet a 4:00 P.M. production deadline.

When Jerome enters, he kicks an empty pizza box into the corner. "You'll have to work somewhere else. I need this conference room."

"I don't know where else we could go," Regina says. "I guess we could move to the cafeteria. What am I going to do with all these notebooks? I don't know how we could move it all. Could you please help?"

SET LIMITS TO UNFAIR TREATMENT.

Fast Fact

Your speech reflects your sense of self. Don't allow bullish behavior to work against you.

Action

The prevailing mode of communication in the business world is confident, assertive, and direct. Therefore, a woman must look and act as though she rightfully belongs.

During childhood, parents use softer, more rapport-building words when talking to girls and aggressive, direct language with boys. Expectations ingrained during childhood often conflict with skills needed as a successful professional adult.

Jerome's behavior inhibits healthy, assertive communication. Therefore, Regina should be confident and direct in response to Jerome's aggressive behavior. Regina will hold her ground with Jerome if she follows these steps:

1. **Identify emotions by a statement of empathy.** "Jerome, I know you are upset and you want this space now."

2. **Follow empathy by stating your assertive right.** "We need to get this job done now and we are unable to move. This space will be available at 4 P.M."

3. **Provide an option, negotiate a win/win situation.** "Or, you can get some people from your department to help us and you can have this room as soon as the project is completed."

Pass the Test with Winning Dialogue

When Margaret announces she's taking early retirement from her management position, Nancy decides she wants to be considered for the vacated job.

"I'm going to apply for Margaret's position," Nancy tells her co-workers. She shares her goals with her family, with her friends at church, and submits her résumé to Steve, the division manager.

Weeks later, Nancy learns Margaret's position has been filled by someone else. She decides to confront Steve while he's walking by her desk.

"Steve, why wasn't I considered for Margaret's position?" she asks.

Steve hesitates. "I'm on my way to a meeting, Nancy. Can we talk about this later?"

Nancy notices everyone is watching her. She rushes into the bathroom, embarrassed.

THE ASSERTIVE PERSON HAS THE SAME RIGHTS AS ANYBODY ELSE.

Fast Fact

The assertive person can see the world from another's perspective, but not at the expense of her own needs. She recognizes the rights of other people, AND asks for what she needs.

Action

Nancy is exhibiting passive-aggressive behavior. In her passive state, she was afraid to ask Steve for the job. Her aggressive confrontational behavior says, "I've got you."

Nancy has a right to know why she didn't get the position. Using assertive behavior, she'll set a definite time to meet with Steve, eliminating interruptions. She begins the conversation something like this:

Nancy: I understand that as our manager, you have the right to promote whomever you wish, and I need some information as to why I wasn't promoted to that position.

Nancy begins with a statement of empathy. She recognizes Steve's rights and asks for what she needs. The word "and" in this transaction is subtle. It gives her needs equal importance.

You've probably received a compliment something like this from a supervisor: "You did a fine job coordinating that project." If you hear the word "but," the strength of the compliment is gone. In assertive communication, you eliminate the word "but" and replace it with the word "and." The more you practice using the word "and," the more you'll be pleased with the results.

Here are some more ways you can reinforce the assertive mode.

♦ Use the word "I." "I want," "I need," "I feel," "It occurs to me."

Aggressive language is "you" language. "You should have," "Why didn't you?" "You always. . . ." People who hear "you" language become defensive. If they are irritated, using "you" makes your statement sound like an accusation.

♦ Use the word "we" to reflect a team's accomplishment. "We did it!" "We made it successful."

♦ Focus on short sentences. Say what you have to say and stop. Women have a tendency to say too much, to build up to the topic, rather than saying specifically what they want.

♦ After you've said what you mean, allow silence to work for you. Radio and television have trained us to feel uncomfortable during silences. Let the other person fill the void.

♦ Speak slowly. When you're using assertive techniques, you're often managing a conflict and feel anxious. When you speak fast, you weaken the intensity of what you have to say. Pause two seconds to get into control. Breathe deeply from your diaphragm to relax your system. This puts you in charge of what you have to say.

♦ Deepen your voice. In assertive, anxious conversations, your voice tones change. Usually women's voices become higher in pitch, making weak, whiny sounds. After you've taken your two-second breath, your voice automatically deepens.

The next time Steve announces an open position, Nancy will use assertive behavior. She'll attend to her needs, submit a résumé to Steve, and make an appointment for an interview.

Tone Up Your Voice and Be Heard

Sarah has a good work record, an excellent education and good managerial skills.

"I feel like I'm doing many things right, but something works against me," she says.

That something is the tone of her voice. Sarah has a sweet little girl voice that sounds weak and whiny.

Andrea has a gentle management style, but she scares her co-workers.

"She always sounds like she's angry," Sarah comments.

GIVE YOURSELF A VOICE TUNE-UP.

Fast Fact

The right words aren't enough. You communicate 38 percent of your message through your tone of voice. You need a voice tone that enhances your message and your image.

Action

"The best money I've spent was on a session with a voice image therapist," Sarah says.

Work with a voice coach or modify your voice by yourself.

Hear ye, hear ye! Here's how to listen for the voice you want:

♦ Put a tape recorder on your desk and forget it's there. Record your voice at least three times during the work day. Record your early morning voice. How do you sound? Is your late morning or mid-afternoon voice different?

♦ Play it back and listen to your speech tones. Notice the things you like and the areas you want to change.

♦ Tape a voice that has the qualities you admire.

♦ Play back this tape and carefully listen to the elements of your model. Be aware of the elements you want to emulate. What makes her speech work? Take your time and listen over and over again. Practice saying the piece with your "model." Then rerecord yourself and notice the changes you've made.

You're not trying to copy someone else's speech. Your goal is to gradually change your tone of voice so you project the confidence and ease that get you the results you want.

Make the Scene with Strong Speech

Maria wants an opportunity to manage a new account. She's been an administrative assistant for the last three years and has seen several co-workers promoted to account manager.

Today, Maria decides to talk to her boss, Suzanne.

"You know, I'd really like to have this project," Maria begins. Suzanne removes her glasses, puts down her pen and invites Maria to sit down in front of her desk.

"I mean, if it's OK with you," Maria says, "but I'm not really sure, all this math and I never really was good at math and all that writing and truthfully, writing isn't my very best thing and, well actually I'm pretty sure I could do it, but. . . ."

DON'T ACT LIKE AN EXTRA WHEN YOU WANT TO BE A STAR.

Fast Fact

Guard against your tendency to undermine yourself.

Action

Project your star quality in every interaction. Here are some ways to assure your leading role.

SPILLPROOFING YOUR PERFORMANCE. Don't reveal too much. If you have a chance at a project that involves math, and you're nervous about your math abilities, don't tell your boss.

Don't Say: "Well, I used to just clam up in math class and my dad would help rne after school and even then, I'm not sure I really learned anything. . . ."

This is spilling conversation. Act spillproof.

Do Say: "I want to help you on this account and I'll need help with the math section. Can you point me in the right direction?"

KEEP IT SHORT. Don't drone on, pouring emotional adjectives everywhere.

Don't Say: "What an absolutely superb, fabulous job you did. . . ."

Do Say: "Great job."

Two words can seem like an exclamation point at the end of a sentence. Keep it short.

DETAILS, DETAILS—BE PRECISE. Avoid vague phrases, wimpy words.

Don't Say: "That was a nice meeting."

Do Say: "You kept the meeting focused, and you appeared to be well-prepared."

Go for clarity and be specific. Use direct language.

ASK QUESTIONS ONLY WHEN YOU MEAN TO. Be confident. Don't make questions out of your statements.

Don't Say: "We'll be able to do this?"

A question on a statement indicates indecisiveness and uncertainty. Don't end a statement with a direct question. "This is a marketing problem, isn't it?" This sounds like you need approval from others to decide whether or not it's a marketing problem.

Do Say: "This is a marketing problem."

Practice dropping your voice at the end of a sentence.

PLEASE, PLEASE DON'T BE TOO POLITE. When you string together a series of polite words, you give others the opportunity to interrupt.

Don't Say: "May I please see that, only for a second, when you're through with it?" Don't be too sweet. Try a direct statement.

Do Say: "I would like to see that, too." Drop your voice. That prompts a short and direct response.

PROJECT CONFIDENCE AND MOVE AHEAD WITH BODY LANGUAGE

Deborah is giving a presentation to her peers. She has worked hard, collecting the data, writing a report that is understandable and information-packed. As she speaks to the group of 20, she crosses her arms over her chest. She stares at the floor, then at the back wall. Her audience rustles in their seat and doodles.

"All that hard work and no one really listened," Deborah complains afterward.

BODY LANGUAGE IS MORE POTENT THAN VERBAL COMMUNICATION.

Fast Fact

Body language influences how people hear your message. Your listeners interpret the meaning of your words through your body language.

Action

You influence people through your body language. This powerful physical communication includes:

- eye contact
- facial expressions
- posture
- gestures

Here's how you can direct your own body language.

THE EYES HAVE IT. Effective eye contact doesn't mean a constant stare. Maintain a relaxed steady gaze about 60% of the time.

- Focus first on the left eye of the person you're speaking with.
- Then focus on the right eye.
- Do this slowly and intently, so you show interest and energy.

You'll feel comfortably connected when you maintain eye contact. If you have weak eye contact, people may think these things about you:

- She's dishonest.
- We can't trust her.
- She lacks confidence or self-esteem.
- She's bored and not interested in me.

If your eye contact is relentless and aggressive, people may think:

- She's evasive.
- She's intimidating.

"When I'm in a negotiating situation, I watch people's eyes," Janet says. "If they keep looking at me, that tells me they're committed and feel confident about their position."

FACE IT. Don't let false smiles get in your way. Girls typically smile more than boys. Women often have an appealing, pleasant and socially responsive look. Usually, this facial expression enhances communication. But it can get in your way.

"My subordinates weren't taking my discipline seriously," Edna said. "I spoke assertively, using the right language, yet I wasn't getting through."

Edna didn't realize she was smiling while she was instructing. That smile weakened her credibility.

BE A STAND-UP. Your posture shows what you think of yourself and what you feel and think about your listener. Take an effective power stance with:

- Straight spine with head erect.
- Feet slightly spread.
- Arms at your side.
- Fingertips curled.

Give assertiveness to your message with an active and erect posture.

ARMED AND POWERFUL. Your gestures denote confidence. Drop your hands to your side. Stand up straight and don't be afraid to take up space. When you take up more space, you appear more powerful.

SITTING SMART. Project confidence even when you're seated. Place your hands in your lap or on the arms of your chair. Keep your feet flat on the floor or crossed at the ankle.

HANDS ON. Always take the initiative at introductions. Stand up when introducing yourself or being introduced.

Extend your hand to both male and female and give them a firm handshake once or twice. Move your arm from the elbow down.

If you receive a limp handshake, ignore and continue your verbal introduction. Or, touch the person's forehead. This encourages him to open his hand slightly and lets you slide your hand in for a firm handshake. This is a warm way of gaining control and of bringing closure to the handshake.

CHECK YOUR "STAR" POWER

It's not only what you say, it's how you say it that reflects your sense of self. What are these people really saying?

1. You are in a meeting. You've made a suggestion and your boss turns away from you, looks at Bill and says, "I'd like to hear something important from you." How do you respond?

   a. "Gary, before we move on, I want to know what part of my message you think is not important." You look directly at your boss, lean forward and use a firm tone of voice.

   b. You push your chair away, sigh and mentally escape.

   c. You chuckle and agree with your boss. "Yeah, my ideas are usually off-the-wall. Can I get you some coffee?"

   d. "Excuse me, Gary," you say. "What I said was important. Don't put me down in front of this group."

2. Joe comes into your office, yells profanity at you in front of others because of a missing report. What do you do?

   a. Hold your ground. Stand up, cross your arms and lean slightly forward and say, "Let's talk about the missing report."

   b. Deny that Joe is in your office. Look away. Pretend he's not there.

   c. Profusely apologize for the missing report.

   d. Scream back at Joe.

3. You have recently been promoted from the ranks. Linda, who has more seniority than you, resents your promotion, and is being uncooperative at every step. How do you react?

a. "Linda, as your supervisor, you can expect fairness and co-operation from me and I expect the same from you. I want to talk about how we can both get our needs met."

b. Avoid contact with Linda. Take the stairs if she's in the elevator. Exclude her from meetings as well as casual conversation.

c. "Linda, I feel so guilty that you didn't get the promotion. Everyone knows you have more seniority. I don't understand why they did this."

d. "Linda, I know you resent my promotion and your present attitude should prove why you didn't get the job."

4. You're a manager in a small company that's on the move. The CFO recently gave you an exceptionally high performance rating, so you're expecting a raise. When you discuss this with him, you're told "the company profit margin is down. You'll have to wait five months." How do you respond?

a. "I appreciate the company's financial situation at this time. I believe my evaluation proved that I am valuable to the company. In five months, I'd like to talk about making the salary increase retroactive."

b. "I'm so sorry to hear about your poor profit margin. Do you think in a few months we'll be able to discuss my salary increase?"

c. "You are right. How insensitive of me. Don't give it another thought."

d. "You're not being fair! I wouldn't have worked so hard if I thought you weren't going to give me a raise."

5. At a working lunch meeting of male colleagues, you are the only female supervisor. You are asked to take notes and keep a fresh pot of coffee brewing. What do you say?

a. "I would prefer someone else take notes and I made coffee at our last meeting. I need to devote my full attention to this meeting."

b. "I'd be happy to act as secretary. Actually, I should have started coffee earlier this morning."

c. "Excuse me. I'm not feeling very well. I don't think I should stay for this meeting."

d. "You're all a bunch of male sexists. I resent your macho implication that women do your menial tasks."

6. You're the project coordinator on a huge sales presentation, but you're doing all the work. Jackie, a co-worker, has shown your slides and printed material to your boss and is taking credit for the material. What do you do?

a. "Both of our names are listed on this project description, yet I'm doing all the work. I'd like to talk to you about sharing the work and the credit."

b. You remain silent. Cream rises to the top, you tell yourself, and quietly resent your boss's lack of appreciation.

c. You decide if Jackie wants all the credit, she can have it. You resign from the project and hope your boss will discover who is the real worker.

d. "You're ignoring this project, yet you're willing to take credit for my work. I'm telling the boss."

7. You inherited a budget that doesn't match your goals, so you're carefully managing your department's consumables. Tony, manager of computer design, is planning a corporate event and requests materials from you. What do you say?

a. "I'm having trouble meeting my budget, Tony. I prefer to not make extra materials available unless it's essential. Tell me about the event and we'll explore some solutions."

b. "I'm sorry, but I'm out of the materials you need. I might be able to help you next week. Is that okay?"

c. "I have no budget to provide these materials for you. I don't make the rules."

d. "You shouldn't ask for more materials! I'm over budget myself. I can't give you anything."

8. Emily, your employee, isn't working up to the goals she agreed upon. When reviewing her performance, you say:

a. "We agreed on certain goals and I've noticed you're having trouble achieving them. Let's discuss choices available in order to improve your performance."

b. "It's obvious the goals we set are too much for you. I'm going to find a job for you that fits your limited abilities."

c. "You know the rough part of my job is, well, I just don't want to hurt your feelings. Do you think we could have a friendly chat about your work?"

d. "You're a sloppy worker. I don't think you care about this job."

GRAND TOTALS

You've learned the four styles of communication:

♦ The *passive* person believes others have more rights than she.

♦ The *aggressive* person believes she has more rights than others.

♦ The *passive-aggressive* person acts like others have more rights, and manipulates others to get her way.

♦ The *assertive* person communicates from a position of equality and believes people have equal rights.

♦ Women have been taught to be passive, to give away personal power by allowing others' needs to come first. You now have the techniques to guard against a learned tendency to undermine yourself.

♦ It's not only what you say, it's how you say it that reflects your sense of self. You've learned how to develop a powerful voice image.

♦ You've clarified your female advantage and taken a close look at the mannerisms and speech habits that can destroy a professional impact.

♦ Body language is more powerful than verbal communication. Make sure your body language says what you mean.

CAPTURING WHAT YOU'VE LEARNED

Things I've learned

_____

_____

Concepts I want to try

_____

_____

Great ideas I want to share with others

_____

_____

Things I want to know more about

_____

_____

Chapter Four

◇

HOW TO CONFIDENTLY DEAL WITH DIFFICULT PEOPLE AND TRYING SITUATIONS

FEAR OF FIGHTING: THE TENACITY TEST

Are you your own white knight, ready to defend and rescue yourself? Do you believe you're worth fighting for? Will you sharpen your words and speak out for yourself? Or are you a wimpy winsome princess, holed up in some dim tower? Test your tenacity with these questing questions.

1. You've had this date planned for weeks—your favorite man, your favorite singer, your favorite band in a special one-night-only concert. You've practically flown through the day. Just as you're ready to leave, your boss shrieks into your office.

   "Emergency," she says. "Our biggest client is flying in from Zurich and I've got a speaking engagement this evening. You're the only person I trust to pick her up." She clasps your hands, looks wildly into your eyes and flies out of the room. What do you do?

a. You call your man and tell him you'll be late for the concert.

b. "NO!" you shout. "I can't do this. I'm busy, too."

c. You follow her and sit across from her in her office, explain your situation and together think of another solution.

2. During an interdepartmental meeting, your boss volunteers you for a huge project. You simply don't have time to do it. What do you do?

a. Grimace and draw a skull and crossbones on your note pad.

b. Speak out and say, "I don't have time for that project right now."

c. After the meeting, get together with your boss and ask her to prioritize your work load for you.

3. For some reason, Cheryl gives you the creeps. Today, you're walking to lunch with friends and she says loudly, "Thought you'd like to know, they're having a purse sale at Wal-Mart." You look down at your purse. It is OLD.

a. You cover your purse with your hands so no one will notice it.

b. Say, "You'll probably want to rush right over to the skin cream sale. I hear they have a new product that practically makes wrinkles disappear."

c. Stop and look at Cheryl. Say, directly, "I'm puzzled. What did you mean just now?"

4. Three people in your department get to take a training class in London. You desperately want to go but doubt your supervisor will think of recommending you.

a. You say to yourself, "I'm not good enough anyway."

b. Stop your supervisor in the hallway and tell her you really deserve that training.

c. Ask your supervisor for an appointment so you can discuss how increasing your training will benefit the company.

5. Your department has worked for weeks on the annual report. You just received copies from the printer and there's a glaring error right on the cover. The printer made the error and you are calling him to have him redo everything when the controller comes into your office, waving the report. He begins a long tirade against you and your department.

   a. You let him go on. He needs to get it out of his system.

   b. You stand up and shout back.

   c. You stand up and say, "I know how upset you are and when you calm down we'll discuss how I solved the problem."

If you totaled any or all As, you're taking the easy way out, giving in, selling out. You need to charge into assertiveness like a woman with a mission.

If you're mainly a B type, you're forceful, using aggressive behavior to make things happen your way. You'll need to hone your chivalry and etiquette so you can get the most from your naturally assertive behavior.

If you chose primarily Cs, your esteem is good. You're willing to consider the other person's needs without giving up your own. This chapter will let you add even more skills for more elegant and assertive workplace effectiveness.

CONFLICT RESOLUTION: HOW TO PROFIT FROM PROBLEM SOLVING

Leila is part of a group that is to develop awareness of the company's new employee benefit plan. She's working with co-workers Ellen, Sam and Fannie.

At their initial meeting, Leila says, "There are so many interesting ways to approach this project. Why don't we take some time and each describe the way we'd most like to work."

Ellen butts in. "We don't have time for a lot of discussion if we want to meet our deadline. We must plunge in and get things done."

"That's the team spirit," Sam says. "Leila, you deal with marketing; Ellen, you get with accounting; and Fannie, you contact human resources," Sam suggests.

"First, I need a current list with everyone's name, title and phone number, then, before I can start listing, I need . . ." Fannie says.

Leila leaves the meeting feeling out of sync, unsuccessful and undervalued. She had no idea her co-workers were so difficult to get along with.

SOMETIMES PEOPLE'S NATURAL DIFFERENCES MAKE THEM SEEM DIFFICULT.

Fast Fact

In most cases people are not difficult; their style just differs from yours. When you're dealing with a difficult person, ask yourself, "How am I contributing to this situation?"

Action

Leila can use her knowledge of the SELF profile to help her understand the different personalities. Then she can match the intensity level of each personality. Many conflicts between people are simply extensions of the SELF profile characteristics. Natural differences in style and communication often cause conflict.

Each personality type on the SELF profile has its own way of dealing with situations, problems and conflicts. Part of being a successful co-worker, employee and manager is understanding the team members' needs, strengths and weaknesses so you can effectively work with them.

For example, Sam, the S type, is spontaneous and controlling. He relishes attention and achievement. He is impatient and doesn't do well with indecision and lack of enthusiasm. His hidden agenda is "Everyone must respect me." When pressured, he attacks.

Ellen, the E person, likes control, responsibility and order. She disdains laziness, ambiguity and emotion. Her secret agenda is, "I must always win." She's autocratic and dogged when under stress. If you tell her to "Do this," she'll wait until the last minute because she feels resentful and unimportant.

Leila, the L type, is a people person. She yearns for community, acceptance and kindness. She cringes at insensitivity, insincerity and dissension. She thinks, "I'll be so unhappy if everyone doesn't like me." If you press her to do something, she'll give in.

Fannie, the F type, likes consistency and information. She tends toward the practical and the perfectionistic. She can't tolerate care-

Figure 4–1

Personalities that criss-cross on the SELF profile have the greatest difficulty understanding each other.

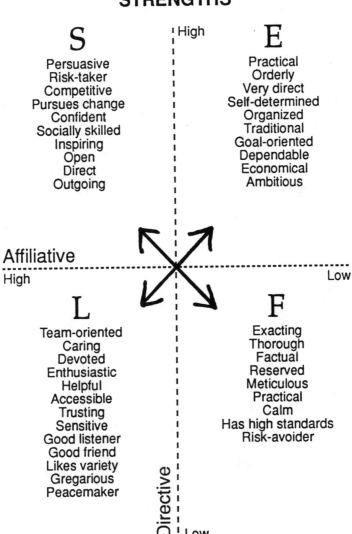

STRENGTHS

S

Persuasive
Risk-taker
Competitive
Pursues change
Confident
Socially skilled
Inspiring
Open
Direct
Outgoing

High

E

Practical
Orderly
Very direct
Self-determined
Organized
Traditional
Goal-oriented
Dependable
Economical
Ambitious

Affiliative

High

Low

L

Team-oriented
Caring
Devoted
Enthusiastic
Helpful
Accessible
Trusting
Sensitive
Good listener
Good friend
Likes variety
Gregarious
Peacemaker

F

Exacting
Thorough
Factual
Reserved
Meticulous
Practical
Calm
Has high standards
Risk-avoider

Directive

Low

lessness, over-assertiveness and arrogance. "It's imperative that I be right," she believes. If conflict blooms, she hurries to avoid it.

It isn't easy understanding, accepting and blending these distinct and different personalities. How can you reduce the tension and blend the needs of this group?

Lowering relationship tensions eases potentially difficult situations. To reduce tension, you can say, "I will give up some of my needs to meet your needs, if you will give up some of your needs to meet mine."

How to Use the SELF Profile to Avoid Conflict

Some SELFs have a natural conflict with other SELFs. But don't beat up on your SELF. You can smooth things out by being aware of the personality profiles and special needs.

S types have a natural conflict with F types. Ss have a buoyancy, a carefree joie de vivre that Fs find hard to abide. For example, here's a dialogue between Sam (S) and Fannie (F):

Sam: "I like to be recognized for my accomplishments."

Fannie: "You're egocentric and bossy."

Sam: "I'm carefree, spontaneous."

Fannie: "You're careless and inconsistent. I, however, am organized."

Sam: "You're a stickler. You have no sense of creativity."

Fannie: "I get the facts and do things right."

Sam: "With your perfectionism, you can't see the whole picture."

E types and L types have difficulty relating to each other. Listen to Ellen (E) and Leila (L) describe themselves.

Ellen: "Someone has to assume the responsibility. I'm glad to do it."

Leila: "You're so controlling. You don't leave space for anyone else."

Ellen: "If we don't keep up to speed, we'll never accomplish what we need to."

Leila: "You rush through everything and don't stop to get others involved. I like to know what other people think."

Ellen: "You're lazy and undisciplined."

Leila: "I think that caring and kindness build a team that can work together."

Ellen: "All these endless conversations. You never get anything done."

Know your personality dimensions, and know the strengths and weaknesses of the people around you. They won't seem nearly as difficult to work with. Understand what you need for psychological safety. Ask for what you need.

Also, understand that other people need to be psychologically safe. Be willing to flex your style to help them meet their needs. Respecting these differences and valuing differences significantly reduces tension.

How to Conquer Your Fear of Conflict

Sally calls Fran into her office.

"Look, I know this is short notice, but I need a spread sheet on this new company, stat." She hands Fran a page of ragged-looking numbers and turns back to her calculator.

"But," Fran says, "I need more information."

"I know this isn't ideal," Sally says. "Do what you have to and get me the spread sheet." Sally punches a number on the telephone.

"There's really no way I can get the numbers to work out with the rest of the . . ." Fran says quietly, not wanting to disturb Sally.

Sally waves her into silence.

Fran leaves, feeling frustrated. "What is wrong with me?" she thinks. She wants to talk more to Sally, but she is afraid Sally will yell at her and think her stupid.

FEAR GETS IN THE WAY OF COMMUNICATION.

Fast Fact
Women are frequently afraid of conflict.

Action

Some of our acculturated beliefs which abet this fear are "Don't rock the boat," "Give in and keep still," or "Peace at any price."

Reframe conflict from a negative to a positive. Every conflict provides an opportunity for growth, an opportunity to enrich a relationship. The opposite of love is apathy, not hate. As long as there is conflict in a relationship, there is energy to work on it. Once apathy has set in, it may be too late.

Fran needs to overcome her fear of conflict and speak out for herself. Every time she lets Sally tromp on her words, Fran loses valuable energy and confidence, and squashes her small reserves of self-esteem.

Women often take things too personally. They allow personal issues to get in the way of the problem. Women tend to internalize. They think, "It must be me. What am I doing wrong?" Dealing with difficult people is a professional issue, not a personal issue.

Fran can ask herself: What is the worst thing that can happen? I won't die. I won't go broke. I probably won't even get fired. Sally may raise her voice.

By writing down these fears, Fran makes them tangible and manageable.

Here's a way to tame your conflict terrors:

♦ Take a sheet of brightly colored paper.

♦ Write all your fears about conflict. Don't edit. Don't be rational. Just write without stopping.

♦ Read your fears aloud, to yourself or to a trusted friend.

♦ When you're done, crumple up the paper and throw it into the corner. Don't pick it up right away. That bright paper is a reminder that you've thrown away your fears.

After Fran does this, she is ready to face Sally with a change in her posture and pacing.

Three Ways to Resolve Conflicts

BE A MIRROR. Carol recently moved from Boston to southern Missouri and opened a craft shop. She had long dreamed of getting out of the rat race of the city and settling into a quiet, friendly town. But she found the townspeople hard to get along with.

"They talk so slowly," she complained to her husband. "I have to talk faster to get them to speed up. But the more interesting and dramatic I act, the more they seem to back off."

YOU FEEL COMFORTABLE WITH PEOPLE WHO ARE LIKE YOU.

Fast Fact

Mirror your difficult person's posture and pacing for a more successful communication effort.

Action

Carol can use her observation of the townspeople to develop a communication style they feel comfortable with.

If they gesture widely, and talk fast and loud, she'll mirror them. If they are quiet and reserved, Carol will tone herself to their level. Mirroring actions eases the tension and increases chances of communication.

How does mirroring help you?

♦ You hold your ground.

♦ You defuse explosiveness.

♦ You make the other person feel comfortable because he or she perceives you are alike.

BE A MODEL. When mirroring is too explosive and intense, you can model behavior. Validate the feelings of the angry person. Say, "I know you're feeling angry and I want to listen, but please sit down. Take a chance to relax."

Keep calm and do not participate in a loud conversation. Instead, say, "I want to talk to you and hear your side, but not like this. Let's get together after things are calm."

BE CLEAR. Just because someone heard what you said, doesn't mean they understood you. Sometimes *intent* is different than *content*. Tell people the reason you want to talk to them. Having enough information naturally reduces tension.

Life Lines for Easing Out of Difficult Situations

1. *Make things objective.*

   You say:　"We both have a problem. Let's find a solution."

   Or:　"I see what you're saying *and* let's explore the alternatives."

Don't say, "but," "yet," or "however," because that negates the first part of the sentence. Notice the difference. "I see what you're saying *but* let's explore the alternatives."

2. *Tread Water.*

When you're angry and too upset to communicate coolly, tread water. Notice something benign. Break the tension with tread talk, such as "Nice suit. Where'd you get it?" Comment on a picture or object. Use small talk to dissipate big tension.

3. *Compliment your adversary.* Be sincere.

Say: "With your great ability to analyze facts, I know we'll come to a great solution."

4. *Think of helping each other stay afloat instead of independently struggling.* What are the advantages of working together? How can you strengthen each other? Concentrate on what you have in common. Focus on this mutual area of benefit. Ask yourself:

   ✦ Do we share any common goals, needs and desires?

   ✦ What's in it for both of us?

   ✦ How can we both get our needs met?

   If you feel your adversary is pushing you into a losing situation, stop. Ask, "How do we both want this conversation to end?"

   Clarify the end-result first, by figuring out what you both want and need. Then you can negotiate and compromise until you reach that goal.

5. Establish comfort. Using your knowledge of the SELF profile, make the other person feel at ease.

DIPLOMATIC SECRETS: NONTHREATENING WAYS TO MAKE CHANGES

One morning something in Emily's office was different. She felt taller. Then she noticed, her cubicle walls were shorter. Emily caught her breath. She'd been demoted overnight. She hurried to the lounge to see if anyone had news about what happened. In the lounge, everyone was upset and nervous. Were their jobs in jeopardy? Was the rumored takeover finally happening?

The branch manager poked in her head. "So, how do you like the bold new designer look?" The room turned coldly quiet. Finally, Emily managed to say, "Fine."

BE AWARE OF SITUATIONS THAT MAKE PEOPLE FEEL NERVOUS, ANXIOUS OR CHALLENGED.

Fast Fact
Change upsets people.

Action
The branch manager has many options for overcoming the staff's natural resistance to change.

Here are some tips for overcoming resistance.

+ Find out how you can relate to people. Use your knowledge of the SELF Profile to help you. Ls and Fs need advance information about change. They're sure to resist negative surprises.

+ Admit the resistance is there. Don't make light of it.

+ Be open and accessible to people.

Speak Easy: Make Confrontation Work for You

Louise is the Director of Nursing in a skilled care facility. Mary is the administrator. Mary sent Louise a memo, notifying her that certain budgets are being reduced. Louise is nervous and upset when she comes into Mary's office to discuss this.

"I can't believe you want to take money away from the patients' entertainment budget," Louise says.

"You don't understand how much it costs to run this place," Mary says.

"But the patients come first," Louise says.

"Exactly. That's why I must have enough for food and housekeeping."

"You act like you don't care about the patients. I know there's another way to cut expenses," Louise says. She storms out of the office, close to tears, feeling unsuccessful and stupid.

FOCUS ON THE PROBLEM RATHER THAN YOUR EMOTIONAL RESPONSE.

Fast Fact

When something bothers you, take ownership of the conflict by owning your feelings.

Action

Louise can safely express her feelings using this simple confrontation model. Mary can use her active listening skills to figure out what is really bothering Louise. Here's how it works.

1. State the facts as you heard them.
2. State your feelings.
3. Explain why you feel that way.

Example:

Fact: When you say you must cut the entertainment budget,

Feeling: I feel frustrated

Whys: because I feel like I'm letting down the patients and their families.

A vital part of assertive behavior is active listening. Repeat what you've heard to show the person you are really listening to them to minimize miscommunications.

Example: Mary says, "You're upset because I might cut the entertainment budget. You feel you'll disappoint the patients and their families."

Louise says, "I'm also worried that not only entertainment but also my salary and my staff are in jeopardy."

Notice how active listening helps ferret out the real problem. Now, develop a resolution. Address the problem with as much information as you have.

Example: Louise says, "I heard you say the reason you're upset is that you're worried your salary and your staff size will be cut. I can assure you, that will not happen. Our accounts receivable are behind this month, so the budget cuts are only temporary."

Notice that throughout this exchange, each woman owned her feelings. "I" statements are important for a successful diplomatic resolution. Remember, another person cannot make you angry, mad, irritated. You allow yourself these feelings.

Turn Clashes into Caucuses

1. **Self Aware:** By mastering the SELF profiles, you gain an understanding of what you and others really want.

2. **Care Full:** Care for others. Reduce relationship tensions by saying, "I'll give up some of my needs to meet your needs, if you'll do the same."

3. **Slow Down and Listen:** Acknowledge and really listen to people's needs. Listen with your eyes. Watch for the nonverbal clues of SELF.

4. **You're in Control:** Remember, nobody makes you feel but yourself. You have control of your feelings. Take mental time out. Breathe deeply. Difficult people don't "make us mad." You allow yourself to feel angry.

5. **You're Great!** Remember how great you truly are. Use personal affirmations, to keep yourself centered and your identity separate from your work. Just because you make a mistake at work does not imply you are a lousy or careless person. It means you made a mistake. Your behavior is separate from your worth as a person.

6. **You Can Do It.** Keep your sense of self-confidence. Affirm your strengths and give yourself a boost.

7. **Share.** Sharing information increases communications. State your intent as well as your content. The more information people have, the more open they are to communication.

Cut Back on Difficult Encounters

To minimize the likelihood of difficult encounters, simply:

- Be warm, approachable and friendly.
- Listen actively.
- Give feedback on what you hear.
- Make people feel important by acknowledging their needs and feelings. Show your willingness to help them meet these needs.

IRONING OUT PROBLEMS: BENEFITS OF CONFRONTATIONS

Claire has been boiling with anger all morning, ever since Stu passed her in the hall and said, "Remember the budget report due this morning?" This was the fourth time this week he'd reminded her. What did he think she was, stupid, forgetful? Didn't he trust her?

She spills coffee on her skirt, fuming. Finally, she decides to go into Stu's office and confront him.

She knocks on the door frame and peers in. "Stu, I'd like to talk to you about why you keep hounding me about deadlines."

Stu looks up from his work and motions her in.

Claire takes a breath and says, "Stu, when you keep reminding me of deadlines, I feel angry and discounted, because I feel you don't trust me to be on time."

Stu looks at Claire. "I hear you saying you feel discounted when I remind you about deadlines. I guess the reason I'm so tense about it, is I've had bad experiences before with my staff not coming through and I pay for it."

CONFRONTING TENSE ISSUES OPENS COMMUNICATIONS.

Fast Fact

When people are willing to explore the reasons for conflict, they open communications and build trust.

Action

Now that Claire and Stu have each expressed themselves, they can resolve their problem. Stu can ask for some system of reassurance that doesn't make Claire feel discounted.

BENEFITS OF MOVING THROUGH CONFLICT:

+ Self-empowerment through self-expression.
+ Team building through open conversation.
+ Fear reduction through communication.
+ Problem solving through confronting issues instead of shoving them aside.

Conflict lets you get closer to people. When you have conflict, you have energy to work on the relationship.

Assert Your Rights: How to Deal with Aggressive Tactics

Deborah's ready for her product presentation with an important new buyer. She's in the restroom, freshening her lipstick, when Cindy waltzes in.

"Boy, I guess you didn't realize it's taboo to wear a beige handbag with those grey shoes," Cindy says.

Deborah gets lipstick on her teeth. She's nervous enough without one of Cindy's snide remarks. She's furious with Cindy but doesn't want to get into an argument.

BE AWARE OF THE PEOPLE YOU FIND DIFFICULT TO BE AROUND.

Fast Fact

The sooner you confront a person you find difficult, the more empowered you feel.

Action

As soon as Deborah's presentation is over, she should talk to Cindy. She'll listen to what Cindy says and respond as though it were genuine.

Deborah: "Your remark in the restroom sounded sarcastic. Was it?"

Cindy: "Can't you take a joke?"

Deborah: "I didn't think it was a joke."

Be assertive and match behavior. Keep asking questions until the issue is resolved.

Just Say "No Way": How to Effectively Handle Negative Behaviors

Kerry drags into Ruth's office and slumps into her boss's desk chair.

"Everything's wrong. I can't believe it—what a day. The entire shipment is screwed up. Everything. I'll never see my husband and child again. I mean, really, I can't believe how much work this will take."

Ruth feels a sense of panic. The shipment was vital to meet deadlines. Now because of everything going askew, her whole production schedule is off.

PEOPLE WITH NEGATIVE BEHAVIOR OFTEN EXAGGERATE PROBLEMS.

Fast Fact

Listen actively to the negative person. Then get down to who, what, where, when, why.

Action

Ruth can ask Kerry specific questions, so Ruth can understand the true nature of the problem.

"Tell me what exactly went wrong?" Ruth might say.

"All the packing numbers were wrong."

"Every one of them?" Ruth asks.

"Well, at least ten and maybe more," Kerry answers.

"Is the merchandise in good shape?" Ruth asks.

"Sure, it's fine. But those numbers can really mess up our books if I don't take care of them."

Once Ruth discovers the true nature of the problem, she can encourage the negative person to solve it herself.

"It sounds like you have a good handle on the situation, Kerry," Ruth says. "Why don't you check all the numbers, correct what's necessary, and then write to the shipper so this problem won't happen again."

How to Get the Strong Silent Type to Open Up

"John, I hear there are some problems in your department. Is this true?"

"No."

"I hear your people are coming in a half hour late."

John doesn't answer.

The strong silent type won't talk or give you information. Maybe he feels embarrassed or wrong. Maybe he doesn't want to hurt your feelings.

Ask open-ended questions, that he can't respond yes or no to. Wait. Watch. Use silence to get his attention and response. "I asked you a question. What's happening?"

If he doesn't respond, set a time limit.

"We only have five minutes."

If he still won't answer, set another meeting for tomorrow.

You may have to take action. "I'll take your silence for a yes."

How to Get the Yes-Woman to Say "No" (or, at Least, "Maybe")

"Sure, you want that by Monday. I'll get it done. You need a 12-page report over the weekend? Well, my brother and his family are coming into town, but I'm sure I'll have time to squeeze it in."

The Yes-woman seeks approval from others rather than herself. She accepts more of the work load than is in her best interest. She thinks "do," before she thinks "delegate."

If she's your boss, ask her to help you prioritize your work load. If she's your employee, say, "I want you as a part of my team. I don't want you too overworked. So when marketing wants something done, check with me before you volunteer."

Tomorrow and Tomorrow and Tomorrow: Dealing with the Procrastinator

Procrastinators want to please everyone but they get nothing done. They need lots of reinforcement.

Give definite deadlines. ASAP means they can put it off. Get a verbal agreement on a time and follow through with a memo that specifies the deadline. Make copies of such memos.

ASAP MEANS IDNY (I DECIDE, NOT YOU)

POWER TOOLS FOR WOMEN

Rose walks by the break room and notices three of her peers, Dave, Mel and Rod, having a cozy cup of coffee. She waves and each of the men nod. After she passes the room, she hears laughter.

Rose touches her hair and twists her wedding ring. In her office, her out-basket is already flowing over. Rose is just two months from her performance review and she's worried her boss will say, "I knew a woman couldn't cut it in this department."

Rose slumps at her desk, and presses her hands against her throbbing forehead. She buzzes for her assistant. The phone isn't picked up.

Mel sticks his head in. "By the way," he says, "I added some things onto the agenda for your meeting Tuesday. I stuck the paper in your basket."

"We're supposed to agree on the agenda as a team," Rose mutters. Mel has already left. She wants to scream at Mel and fire her secretary. She feels she's caught in the middle of something so unwieldy and so large, she can never be successful.

ASSESS THE SITUATION. IS IT A DIFFICULT PERSON OR SITUATION?

Fast Fact

Don't get emotionally involved. Notice your response and analyze why you respond that way.

Action

Rose is caught in a situation where she feels like she's being criticized, put down, back-stabbed, and ridiculed. She'd like to burst into rage and tears, but knows someone would comment, "What else do you expect from a woman?"

Here is the list of power tools, or behaviors, that can help you deal with similar, difficult situations and people.

How to Put Up with Put-Downs and Criticism

1. *Disarming.* When someone is hostile, repeat word for word what the hostile person said. Ask, "I want to make sure I didn't misunderstand you." Center yourself. See yourself tall, calm, strong. That lowers the tension.

2. *Cut those hedges.* When she says, "You know I'd never tell you what to do, but . . ." you say, "Thanks. I appreciate that."

3. *Honey do.* When he says, "Even a woman can do that," you say, "When did you start feeling women were inferior?"* When he says, "Honey, get me that fax," say, "Bob, I am uncomfortable when you call me honey and I'm sure you didn't mean anything by it. I want to be called by my name." He says, "My, aren't you sensitive." Repeat your request simply and briefly,

---

* This is a technique similar to the one Suzette Haden Elgin uses in THE GENTLE ART OF SELF-DEFENSE.

taking the focus off the unrelated issue of sensitivity. Say, "I may be sensitive sometimes and I do want to be called by my name."

4. *Call to criticize.* If you need to criticize, couch your comments in positive terms. Example: "I really appreciate how clean you're keeping your desk and you can help me even more by answering the phone by the fifth ring."

What to Do When You're Challenged

Use anger positively:

+ Make eye contact.
+ Posture or mirror the other person's body language.
+ Watch word choice. Own your sentences.
+ Be specific; mention specific incidents.
+ Be receptive.

Stay in control:

+ Know your SELF. Breathe deeply. The difference between fear and courage may be a deep breath.
+ Learn to stop your behavior.
+ Deal with your feelings.
+ Don't blame anyone.
+ Keep the focus on problem/solution.

No More Tears: How to Avoid Crying When You're Angry

You're in an important meeting and someone makes a snide remark about your performance. Tears well up and you're terrified you'll cry.

+ Don't panic.
+ Tilt your head back slightly. Lowering your head invites tears.
+ Take a time out. Leave the room. Don't ask for permission.

- Take a quick walk and some deep breaths to regain composure.

- If you can't leave the room, distract yourself. Focus on something in the room and take deep breaths to relax yourself. Pull out a file. Move around. Pour yourself a cup of coffee. Sharpen a pencil. Take a mental get-away. Imagine you're in a green bubble that filters out negative energy. Physical movement calms you.

How to Deal with Back-Stabbers

This is the third time your co-worker Andy has warned you that John is saying degrading things about you when you're out of town.

You trust Andy and know her information is valid. You need to confront John.

Use a firm tone of voice, eye contact and assertive body language.

Say, "John, it's been brought to my attention that you've been saying negative things about me behind my back. If it's true, I am offended and I do want it stopped."

"Who told you that?" John asks.

You repeat, "If it's true, I am offended and I do want it stopped."

If John pushes you for more information, use the following phrase as a segue to keep the focus on the problem at hand.

Say, **"The subject is not . . . ,"** followed by, **"the subject is. . . ."**

In John's case, you'd say, "The subject is not who told me. The subject is your back-stabbing behavior."

How to Handle Ridicule

At one time you felt lucky to be a blond. Blond jokes may make you feel ridiculed.

If the jokes are generic, you may choose to ignore them.

If the ridicule gets personal, then confront the offender by saying the facts, your feelings and what you need.

Fact: When you tell a joke about me

Feeling: I feel ridiculed and hurt

Need: and I need for you to stop telling jokes at my expense.

DEFUSING TIME BOMBS: HOW TO TAKE THE HEAT OUT OF CONFRONTATIONS

Dino comes into Audrey's office, shaking a folder at her.

"The Clemson file is late again," he says.

"I just got the numbers yesterday," Audrey says. She scoots her chair back so she can keep her distance from the frenzied, pacing Dino.

"No excuses," Dino shouts. "I need these updated by the first and I don't care how it happens." He throws the folder on the floor and glares at Audrey.

DON'T FIGHT WITH A BULLY.

Fast Fact
Bullies love to fight and will always win.

Action
Audrey needs to find out what's going on. Is he really upset about the file or is there something else? She will stand up and say firmly, "Excuse me, Dino. I know this file is important. I want to talk this out with you. And I'm not willing to discuss it like this." She stands and waits for him to leave her office. If he doesn't, she walks out.

Pacing and posturing are crucial when dealing with explosive behaviors. Match their intensity and volume.

If they apologize, don't forgive them. If you forgive them, they'll have permission for another tantrum.

Say, "I want to talk to you and I'm not willing to discuss it like this." Say this as many times as you need to.

How to Take the Sting Out of High-Voltage Communications

Don't be surprised if you have to practice to perfect your new high-voltage communication style.

Start by thinking of a behavior type that is difficult for you. Your manager criticizes you in a meeting. What do you do? Clam up? Pout? Complain to co-workers?

Think of why you respond a certain way and how you would prefer to respond. Practice finding a new response. Write it out. Rehearse it, looking into the mirror. Work on assertive posture and voice tone. Then try out your new behavior on a friend or choose another safe time to try out your new behavior.

THE ASSERTIVENESS CHALLENGE

You now have the tools to face conflict fearlessly. How does the new assertive you face each of these challenges?

1. You've had this date planned for weeks—your favorite man, your favorite singer, your favorite band in a special one-night-only concert. You've practically flown through the day. Just as you're ready to leave, your boss shrieks into your office.

    "Emergency," she says. "Our biggest client is flying in from Zurich and I've got a speaking engagement this evening. You're the only person I trust to pick her up." She clasps your hands, looks wildly into your eyes and flies out of the room. What do you do?

    a. You call your man and tell him you'll be late for the concert.

    b. "NO!" you shout. "I can't do this. I'm busy, too."

    c. You follow her and sit across from her in her office, explain your situation and together think of another solution.

2. During an interdepartmental meeting, your boss volunteers you for a huge project. You simply don't have time to do it. What do you do?

    a. Grimace and draw a skull and crossbones on your note pad.

    b. Speak out and say, "I don't have time for that project right now."

    c. After the meeting, get together with your boss and ask her to prioritize your work load for you.

3. For some reason, Cheryl gives you the creeps. Today, you're walking to lunch with friends and she says loudly, "Thought you'd like to know, they're having a purse sale at Wal-Mart." You look down at your purse. It is OLD.

   a. You cover your purse with your hands so no one will notice it.

   b. Say, "You'll probably want to rush right over to the skin cream sale. I hear they have a new product that practically makes wrinkles disappear."

   c. Stop and look at Cheryl. Say, directly, "I'm puzzled. What did you mean just now?"

4. Three people in your department get to take a training class in London. You desperately want to go but doubt your supervisor will think of recommending you.

   a. You say to yourself, "I'm not good enough anyway."

   b. Stop your supervisor in the hallway and tell her you really deserve that training.

   c. Ask your supervisor for an appointment so you can discuss how increasing your training will benefit the company.

5. Your department has worked for weeks on the annual report. You just received copies from the printer and there's a glaring error right on the cover. The printer made the error and you are calling him to have him redo everything when the controller comes into your office, waving the report. He begins a long tirade against you and your department.

   a. You let him go on. He needs to get it out of his system.

   b. You stand up and shout back.

   c. You stand up and say, "I know how upset you are and when you calm down we'll discuss how I solved the problem."

GRAND TOTALS

You now have the tools you need to deal with difficult people and difficult situations. You have the body language and the words to be knowledgeable, assertive and successful in a difficult business situation.

+ You have learned that natural differences often make people appear difficult.

+ You have tools to overcome your fear of conflict. You know that fear gets in the way of communication understanding.

+ Using the SELF profile, you understand the needs for each personality type and the challenges of each. You know who will cause you the most difficulty and how to deal with them.

+ You know how to stay in control and deal with aggressive tactics.

CAPTURING WHAT YOU'VE LEARNED

Things I've learned

Concepts I want to try

Great ideas I want to share with others

Things I want to know more about

Chapter Five

◇

KNOW THE RULES, PLAY THE GAME
Effective Use of Organizational Politics

Do you have what it takes to compete? Do you pore through procedure manuals to get a clear picture of what's expected of you? Do you hang out at the water cooler and soak in the loosey goosey about George's department?

ARE YOU A TEAM PLAYER? TEST YOUR SKILLS

Try this quiz and find out whether you're a team player or headed for the bench.

1. "You want something done? Ask a busy person," your boss says as he tosses a file on your desk. "Let me know when you can finish this cost analysis." What do you do?

a. Call Fred, the numbers cruncher in Accounting who always has food stains on his chin. Call Bernice in Computers, then call Donna in Word Processing. Forget that she sounds like the exorcist from *Poltergeist.* Tell them your boss is in a pinch and he always remembers those who pitch in.

b. Stuff the file in your briefcase and work evenings on the analysis. Your boss knows you're an overachiever.

c. Do the cost analysis. But first, call your friend in bookkeeping, meet her at the vending machines and tell her, "My boss is the laziest. I heard he's going to get a one-way ticket out the front door."

2. You have six days to produce a brochure for your accounting firm. You need to gather information, establish a distribution list, design the brochure and write copy. Tomorrow, you're supposed to be in Milwaukee for three days. What do you do?

a. Turn the job over to a reliable vendor, even though they're not on your company's list of preferred vendors. If someone accuses you of overlooking policy, say, "I didn't realize it was a problem. I was under a tight deadline. I knew these vendors could get the job done for us."

b. Take the brochure file with you, write the copy in your motel room, find a starving freelance designer in Milwaukee who will work overtime to help you.

c. Pore over the *Policies and Procedures* manual to see which vendors your company will approve. Then call Marge in Word Processing and say, "Whoever selects vendors in this company has no design taste, whatsoever."

3. In the advertising department, you and Don have worked closely on a national account. Together, you'll present your ad campaign to their Portland headquarters. If you travel together, you're afraid people will spread rumors about your relationship. What should you do?

a. Tell co-workers you're working with Don on the account. Tell them where you're going and where you'll be staying, in case they need to reach you.

b. Thank Don for offering to mentor you. Tell him that while you're in the office, you need to be seen working alone to avoid stories.

c. Hang out at the water cooler and start a rumor about the marketing vice-president.

4. During your hour lunch break, you stop to pick up a few things at a clothing specialty store. When you arrive, it seems other shoppers had the same idea. What do you do?

a. Say to the clerk, "I have 30 minutes. I know what I want. Do you have time to work with me?"

b. Tell yourself you hate crowds, spend the time in the food court sipping a cola, and read the newspaper.

c. Take names of clerks who simply sit around and do nothing. Show the floor manager your list.

5. The loosey goosey about George's department is that his #2 manager plans to resign. This is a coveted position, one that is pivotal to your career. What will you do to get it?

a. Hang out at the water cooler. Take gossip seriously. Plan a strategy, time and place to talk to George. Position yourself as a viable candidate for the job.

b. Your good work should speak for itself. Expect to be noticed, and it will happen.

c. Tell others the job is an absolute nightmare so they'll stay away from it.

6. You've tried everything to get along with Rachel, your boss. You've talked to her about work issues, you've asked others for advice on how to work with Rachel, you've even attended training classes. But no matter what you do, it isn't enough. How can you win her over?

a. Cut your losses. Move on. You can't outlast a bad boss.

b. Stay late. Come in early. Make sure she sees your full briefcase each night as you walk out.

c. Become her eyes and ears. Tell her what you heard at the lunchroom.

7. You dress according to the corporate culture. You're the best technical writer in the department, yet you can't understand why you're consistently overlooked for a promotion. What can you do?

   a. Showcase your other talents. Develop greater ease talking about your skills and accomplishments in other areas. Seek a mentor who can help you move out of your seemingly dead-end position.

   b. Change your fashion image, place a personal ad in the business section, rearrange your office furniture.

   c. Make photocopies of your checking account's balance. Distribute them among managers with a note, "Could you live like this?"

8. You brought in 150 new customers during the last quarter, topping the quota by a record 21 percent. How will you get people to notice your accomplishments?

   a. Keep a log of your new customers. Submit a weekly updated report to your boss. Talk about the strategies you need to increase customers. Write an article for the newspaper on how to increase sales.

   b. Next quarter, reach 28 percent. You're sure to be noticed.

   c. Post sales reports in the bathroom, put them in the lunchroom. Call your friends. Speak loudly as you share the news.

SCORING

How did you feel about corporate competition? Do you like it? Hate it? Are you indifferent to it?

If you scored all As, you're a team player. You focus on individual strengths, yours and those of your co-workers. You know how to be taken seriously. Bottom line, you understand that you are in charge of your own advancement. You are savvy, self-assured and you stay on track. In this chapter, you'll learn how to make the most of your team-member skills.

If you scored Bs, you're the office martyr, a Joan of Arc, trying to do everything yourself. You're playing an individual sport and are destined to end up on the bench. Stop doing it alone. You're worth the recognition you deserve! Read on.

If you scored Cs, people depend on you for gossip, not leadership. People want the inside scoop. But they seldom trust the person scooping it out. In this chapter, you'll find out how to get on the inside loop.

HOW TO POSITION YOURSELF AS A TEAM MEMBER

Brooke believes that with sheer determination, late night meetings, and a comprehensive media plan, she can draw 150 people to the company's investment seminar.

Zeke, one of her committee members, recommends names of people from different departments to sit in on the meetings. "We could use their opinions. They'll be important in passing the word."

"But will they do any work?" Brooke asks.

"In this case, work isn't the issue. It's important you include them," Zeke answers.

"I hate office politics," Brook says. "If they're not going to help, why let them serve on my committee?"

UNDERSTANDING OFFICE POLITICS SAYS YOU KNOW WHAT IT TAKES TO COMPETE.

Fast Fact
A team player maximizes individual strengths.

Action
Women tend to go it alone, do everything "by the book," be all things to all people. During childhood, a girl plays with people she likes, people who know how to share, take turns, be polite, people who make her feel good. If her friends don't play the way she plays, she goes home.

Boys play to accomplish a goal.

David loves to play soccer, but doesn't like Jason, the team's goalie. Jason's taller, he lives in a different part of town, and hangs around with people David doesn't like. Jason and David frequently get into fights at school.

But while they're on the field, David has to depend on Jason to block the ball so that the team will win. Every soccer point is the result of several players working together to set up the goal.

At work, men establish relationships to reach their personal and group goals. "He's the guy who pulls the ropes. I'll take him to lunch." Strategizing, building a strong network of allies, is part of their problem-solving skills.

You can also build strong allies. Get key people to support and help you reach your goals. Here's what you can do to create team-building relationships and position yourself as a valuable member of the team.

♦ Analyze your goal. Make a list of things you can do and things you can't do, then decide who you can depend on to help you reach your goal.

♦ Analyze your co-workers' individual strengths.

♦ Seek out people who have solved problems similar to yours, even if they are different from you. You don't have to like them, but you do have to know if you can rely on them.

♦ Get people to participate on your team by meeting their psychological needs. Invite a person who likes to work with numbers to be your committee's financial wizard.

♦ Show appreciation. People with the most powerful positions always give credit to others.

♦ Take blame if things don't go well. Co-workers will rush to work with you. They know failure is an organizational problem more than a personal issue.

♦ Keep your ego off the team. You're the most powerful person in a meeting if you quietly wait until others have voiced their opinions. Then, you'll know how to respond.

♦ Keep scores from results only. Measure results, not activities.

♦ Talk about the results you've accomplished and issue weekly reports to your management about these results. Be sure to keep a copy in your personal file and take it with you at performance appraisal time.

♦ Maintain self-respect. It's more important than being liked.

♦ Plug into the grapevine. Find out who should be on your team.

♦ Keep your responses predictable. Don't overlook an employee's missed deadline one month, then raise hell over a delay the next month.

Get Rid of the Fear of Speaking Up

The success of every team is dependent upon the strength of each member. Your co-workers depend on you for your ideas. If fear prevents you from stating your position, then your team loses because they didn't get to hear your idea.

To be an active communicating part of your team, consider some of these strategies.

1. Imagine your frustration at the end of a meeting if you had something to say, and didn't say it. Here are eight rules to help you prepare for that meeting, so that you don't experience frustrations.

   ♦ Write down your ideas before you say them.

   ♦ Organize your thoughts.

   ♦ Research the issue in advance.

   ♦ Know where you stand on each issue.

   ♦ Share your ideas. Find out who will support you.

   ♦ Find out who may oppose your position.

   ♦ Work out a strategy in advance with your opposition.

   ♦ Minimize negative surprises. Do creative "what if" thinking.

2. "You can't be all things to all people. But you can be someone great to some people," says Lisa Valenti, business consultant and international presenter. "Present your ideas to the right people, those who enhance your credibility, those who are willing to represent your ideas."

   As a woman, you may be excluded from some male arenas where discussion of major issues leads to crucial decisions. These arenas might include the Saturday golf game or drinks after work. Connect with a strong male counterpart who will represent your ideas in that arena. Choose someone you trust to give you credit and the feedback you need. Help other people help you reach your goals.

Know the Rules, Then Be Creative About When to Break Them

AnnaLise flies first class to Boston to present a creativity seminar. On the flight, she meets a woman who needs help brainstorming for marketing ideas. While AnnaLise is in town, she and the woman have dinner twice at very nice restaurants.

Two weeks after she returns, Adam in Accounts Payable marches into her office. "You know what your problem is? You never read the procedure manual. We don't fly first class in this company. That's what it says right here, page 48," he says, tapping the book.

"I didn't realize the policy was that definite," AnnaLise says. "I'm glad you brought that page to my attention. My best client contacts come from the first class section and I have several new customers because of those contacts. I prefer flying first class for that reason and I'll be happy to give you the facts and figures that show how these contacts have brought money to the company. Then, perhaps we can discuss the possibility of my continuing with this upgrade on some flights."

GO AFTER THE RESULTS FIRST. IT'S EASIER TO ASK FOR FORGIVENESS.
THEN, SEEK PERMISSION.

Fast Fact

Creativity is no longer a frill; in the 1990s, creative problem solving is a survival skill.

Action

Women frequently feel uncomfortable taking action before asking permission. You were taught to ask first, then if no one objected, you could proceed.

If you are compelled to do things the "right way," you cannot dream up results-oriented solutions. As a creative, flexible worker, you add strength to a team.

- To motivate a non-team player, help them do what you want them to do because they want to do it.
- If you're attacked by a policies person, smile confidently. Find out what motivates them and assure them you are focused on the same outcome. Clarify that outcome and proceed with confidence.
- Be optimistic. Keep your body language open and friendly.
- Thank the attacker for taking concerns to you. Take those concerns and immediately focus on solutions. Position yourself as a problem-solver, not a problem identifier.

Tap into Informal Channels of Information

To Carmella, the break room seems disorganized. One morning, she moves the coffee maker next to the sink, the tables away from the refrigerator, and replaces the old microwave with a new digital model.

Richard, her boss, gasps when he sees the room. "You can't move things around. That isn't the way we do things around here. And put the microwave back before anyone finds out you've moved it."

Later, Carmella learns that the microwave is a gift from Ernest Swanson, one of the company's founding fathers who died suddenly two years ago, leaving a trail of loyal employees behind.

KNOW YOUR COMPANY'S ORAL HISTORY.

Fast Fact

Knowing the roots of your organization is a powerful communication tool.

Action

How much time have you spent getting to know your company's oral history? How did top management get to where they are now? Take some time to get the inside scoop on who's who in your company. Here are some questions to ask:

+ Who started the company?
+ Who made it to the top?
+ Who died along the way?
+ Why did they die along the way?
+ Did managers come up from the ranks, or were they brought in from other companies?
+ Who will support your idea?
+ Who should you get on your team?
+ Who starts the rumor? Who feeds it?

Use what you learn to position yourself on the team, to strengthen your negotiations, and to show management your leadership skills.

When Carmella puts together her next task force, she'll know Ernest Swanson's management style and who's copying it. She'll know who liked to work with him, and to whom he bequeathed inside information.

Don't Let Yourself Get Pigeon-Holed

Computer manuals, which Rosette has written, line the bookshelves in her office. Anyone can see what a prolific technical writer she is.

While she's on break, Rosette stirs cream into her coffee when she overhears her boss say, "We're splitting the department and I'll be placing an ad in the paper for a new director. Do you know any one?"

Rosette rushes out of the break room and calls her best friend. "After everything I've done for this company. I'm sitting right there, and she doesn't even think about me. I've been here for eight years. How can she do this to me?"

Her friend, Janet, is an assistant VP for a competitor. "Maybe you're too indispensable. Show them what else you can do."

WHEN YOU EXCEL AT YOUR JOB, MANAGEMENT TENDS TO PIGEON-HOLE YOU IN THAT POSITION.

Fast Fact
You will move up the corporate ladder when you show management all your skills.

Action
You're working in a society where you need to balance being a specialist against becoming too specialized.

In her SE!F Profile series, Sally Jenkins, business and communications consultant, says women need to know something about lots of topics. They need to be "cluster specialists." Try some of these ideas to get out of your specialty rut.

♦ Enroll in classes at a community college or get an undergraduate or graduate degree. Most employers provide a tuition reimbursement plan.

♦ Make yourself visible to your boss. Let your boss know what you're doing to advance yourself personally and professionally.

♦ Raise your visibility outside your company. Use your professional network to let collegues know what you're doing. Word will either get back to your boss, or another company will want to hire you.

◆ Keep the big team picture in mind. Know what you want to do, tell collegues what you want, then find ways to accomplish it.

Make the Most of the Grapevine

When Nadine sees Carole, Martha, Brandon and Richard heading for the water cooler, she grabs her cup and follows them.

"Bob's quitting," Carole says. "I just typed his resignation."

"Wow," Nadine says. "What do you think will happen?"

"Think?" Carole sips water. She looks over her shoulder, leans close to Brandon and Richard. "I already know. Next month, I'm putting an ad in the paper."

"No kidding," Nadine says. "What are they looking for?"

Carole starts to answer, then waits while Alice from Accounting walks past.

"Well, some of us have work to do," Alice says.

Nadine smiles. Poor Alice hasn't a clue about office politics.

"IF YOU LEARNED ABOUT SOMETHING FROM YOUR BOSS *BEFORE* YOU LEARNED ABOUT IT FROM THE GRAPEVINE, YOU HAVE A GAP IN YOUR INTELLIGENCE SYSTEM."
—MARILYN MOATS KENNEDY, PRESIDENT, CAREER STRATEGIES

Fast Fact

Eighty percent of what you hear by the grapevine is true. There's more to get at the coffee station than coffee!

Action

Each organization is governed by two types of power: *formal* and *informal*.

Formal power consists of rules, regulations, flow charts, policies and procedures manuals.

Informal power lies within rumor mills, grapevines and interpersonal relationships.

A grapevine is a cluster of four to six people. Every gossip cluster has an information leader, a person who has *real* power and can cause something to change. This person could be anyone in the organization, from support personnel to the president, depending on the cluster's purpose and strategy.

Women tend to dismiss gossip clusters as office politics. Men see gossip clusters as an opportunity to develop professional strategies.

- Make a deliberate choice to be part of one of these grapevines.
- Decide how often you need to be in touch with the people in your grapevine.
- Respect the information. Keep it within your cluster. People within each cluster establish a bond of trust. They know if they give you information, you won't run to another grapevine, and you won't break up the grapevine you're in.
- You are not the information leader. You're the listener, the person who says, "No kidding," "Wow, how'd you find out about that?" or "That's fascinating."
- Each person comes to the gossip cluster with a goal and so should you.
- Use the knowledge to position yourself with the company.
- Then ask, how do I strategize myself to reach my goals? Am I relying enough upon others?

Here's what you can do to position yourself for a job opening.

- Take the person who's leaving out to lunch. Say, "I heard through the grapevine that you're thinking about leaving. Help me learn the ropes. I'd be honored to be considered as your replacement. How can I make that happen?"
- Make yourself visible to the person hiring. Let the boss know you'd like to be considered, and why you're right for the job.
- Ask the boss what else you need to do to be better prepared for the position and work out a plan that shows your willingness to take on additional training and responsibilities.

Toot Your Own Horn

In the last few months, Joanna successfully managed a video project and placed four articles in major magazines.

Larry, her boss, was reading a magazine article when he accidentally noticed her by-line and called her on the phone.

"I didn't know you'd written this," Larry said. "It's fabulous. What else do you do?"

"Oh, just little stuff. PTA, Mother's March of Dimes, and I produced a $50,000 video for marketing."

Larry laughed. "Is there anything else you'd like to point out to me?"

YOU ARE THE ONLY ONE TOTALLY IN CHARGE OF YOUR OWN ADVANCEMENT. BECOME YOUR OWN PUBLIC RELATIONS AGENCY.

Fast Fact

Women have been taught to be nice, don't make waves, don't show off. Yet, they dominate the public relations field by promoting others in the media.

Action

For women, good isn't good enough. You need to be outstanding. Have a proven track record of your performance. Here's how to do that.

♦ *Talk about your accomplishments.* Weave them into conversations. Often when women receive compliments, they point out the flaw within the compliment.

> Don't say: "Thanks, I was just lucky" when you can say "Thanks, I put a lot of time and effort into the project and used my organizational skills to pull it together."

♦ *Keep a weekly list of your activities.* Make copies of them, take them to your boss, and say, "I know you are busy and your time is limited, so I'm putting together a weekly report of my accomplishments to keep you informed of my meeting goals and progress on projects." Make a copy of those accomplishments. Drop a copy in your personal folder and take it with you at performance review time.

Lists also let you see what you've accomplished, especially when you feel like you've had a day when you couldn't get anything done.

♦ *Become your own public relations firm.* When Sally was in the banking industry, she developed a series of financial seminars for women. Some of the topics included ways to manage assets, trusts and deposits.

A non-team player would have taken the idea to her boss and said, "Boss, do you have a minute?" or "You may not be interested, but . . ."

Sally tucked her seminar file under her arm, went into her boss's office and said, "Boss, how would you like to have some of the women's money that's floating around Kansas City?"

She had a plan worked out, contacts lined up, and then she made her plan happen.

When her boss gave her the go-ahead, Sally called the newspaper and offered to do an article series on how women manage their assets.

If you don't like to write, offer to be a newspaper resource for an article on women managing their assets. The secret to being an article resource is to call and introduce yourself to the editor.

HOW WELL DO YOU PLAY THE POLITICAL GAME?

Use your political savvy to guide you through these problems.

1. "You want something done? Ask a busy person," your boss says as he tosses a file on your desk. "Let me know when you can finish this cost analysis." What do you do?

   a. Call Fred, the numbers cruncher in Accounting who always has food stains on his chin. Call Bernice in Computers, then call Donna in Word Processing. Forget that she sounds like the exorcist from *Poltergeist*. Tell them your boss is in a pinch and he always remembers those who pitch in.

   b. Stuff the file in your briefcase and work evenings on the analysis. Your boss knows you're an over-achiever.

   c. Do the cost analysis. But first, call your friend in bookkeeping, meet her at the vending machines and tell her, "My boss is the laziest. I heard he's going to get a one-way ticket out the front door."

2. You have six days to produce a brochure for your accounting firm. You need to gather information, establish a distribution list, design the brochure and write copy. Tomorrow, you're supposed to be in Milwaukee for three days. What do you do?

   a. Turn the job over to a reliable vendor, even though they're not on your company's list of preferred vendors. If someone accuses you of overlooking policy, say, "I didn't realize it was a problem. I was under a tight deadline. I knew these vendors could get the job done for us."

b. Take the brochure file with you, write the copy in your motel room, find a starving freelance designer in Milwaukee who will work overtime to help you.

c. Pore over the *Policies and Procedures* manual to see which vendors your company will approve. Then call Marge in Word Processing and say, "Whoever selects vendors in this company has no design taste, whatsoever."

3. In the advertising department, you and Don have worked closely on a national account. Together, you'll present your ad campaign to their Portland headquarters. If you travel together, you're afraid people will spread rumors about your relationship. What should you do?

a. Tell co-workers you're working with Don on the account. Tell them where you're going and where you'll be staying, in case they need to reach you.

b. Thank Don for offering to mentor you. Tell him that while you're in the office, you need to be seen working alone to avoid stories.

c. Hang out at the water cooler and start a rumor about the marketing vice-president.

4. During your hour lunch break, you stop to pick up a few things at a clothing specialty store. When you arrive, it seems other shoppers had the same idea. What do you do?

a. Say to the clerk, "I have 30 minutes. I know what I want. Do you have time to work with me?"

b. Tell yourself you hate crowds, spend the time in the food court sipping a cola, and read the newspaper.

c. Take names of clerks who simply sit around and do nothing. Show the floor manager your list.

5. The loosey goosey about George's department is that his #2 manager plans to resign. This is a coveted position, one that is pivotal to your career. What will you do to get it?

a. Hang out at the water cooler. Take gossip seriously. Plan a strategy, time and place to talk to George. Position yourself as a viable candidate for the job.

b. Your good work should speak for itself. Expect to be noticed, and it will happen.

c. Tell others the job is an absolute nightmare so they'll stay away from it.

6. You've tried everything to get along with Rachel, your boss. You've talked to her about work issues, you've asked others for advice on how to work with Rachel, you've even attended training classes. But no matter what you do, it isn't enough. How can you win her over?

a. Cut your losses. Move on. You can't outlast a bad boss.

b. Stay late. Come in early. Make sure she sees your full briefcase each night as you walk out.

c. Become her eyes and ears. Tell her what you heard at the lunchroom.

7. You dress according to the corporate culture. You're the best technical writer in the department, yet you can't understand why you're consistently overlooked for a promotion. What can you do?

a. Showcase your other talents. Develop greater ease talking about your skills and accomplishments in other areas. Seek a mentor who can help you move out of your seemingly dead-end position.

b. Change your fashion image, place a personal ad in the business section, rearrange your office furniture.

c. Make photocopies of your checking account's balance. Distribute them among managers with a note, "Could you live like this?"

8. You brought in 150 new customers during the last quarter, topping the quota by a record 21 percent. How will you get people to notice your accomplishments?

a. Keep a log of your new customers. Submit a weekly updated report to your boss. Talk about the strategies you need to increase customers. Write an article for the newspaper on how to increase sales.

b. Next quarter, reach 28 percent. You're sure to be noticed.

c. Post sales reports in the bathroom, put them in the lunch-room. Call your friends. Speak loudly as you share the news.

GRAND TOTALS

Women tend to go it alone. But isolation puts you on the bench when others are strengthening bonds as team players. Here's what you can do to be part of the team.

- ◆ Analyze your individual strengths and weaknesses. Decide who you can lean on to make the team look strong.

- ◆ Go after the results first. Use your creative skills to solve problems. There are times when asking for forgiveness, then seeking permission, is the best approach.

- ◆ Use all your informal channels of information: grapevine, gossip clusters, mentors and networking. Remember, if you're learning the inside scoop from your boss, you have a gap in your information system.

- ◆ Toot your own horn when you do a job well. Don't become indispensable when you have skills and knowledge to do many things.

CAPTURING WHAT YOU'VE LEARNED

Things I've learned

_____

_____

Concepts I want to try

_____

_____

Great ideas I want to share with others

_____

_____

Things I want to know more about

_____

_____

Chapter Six

◇

MAKING YOUR IDEAS WORK: THE ART OF SUCCESSFUL NEGOTIATIONS

WHY YOUR OWN "SWEET WAY" WON'T WORK

"Don't be selfish."

"Think of other people first."

"Don't take more than your share."

It's time to let go of female fictions and face the facts: If you don't ask for what you want, if you aren't prepared to be *visible, vocal and vibrant,* you won't be successful.

Test Your Communication Style

Are you a *collapser,* a *collaborator* or a *competitor?*

1. You proposed a new way of marketing your company's service. Your boss, Daryl, who has had your proposal for several weeks,

finally calls you into his office. "This proposal definitely has merit. But it's just not economically feasible," he says. How do you respond?

   a. You lower your eyes and say quietly, "Thanks for considering it."

   b. You say, "That proposal describes just one of many ways we could revitalize marketing. I have other ideas I'd like to tell you about."

   c. "You don't fully understand the depth of that marketing proposal. I have considered every aspect. In the long run, that marketing plan will make us a lot of money."

2. Employee morale is low in your company. You want your boss to give the employees a party and authorize a casual dress day once a week. You're making notes, trying to think of the right time and way to approach him. His secretary comes into your office and says, "What are you working on so diligently?" You say:

   a. "Nothing important."

   b. You tell her about your project and ask her advice.

   c. You cover your papers with both hands and say, "It's top secret."

3. For two hours you and your co-worker Ron have been trying to choose a new company logo. You have 20 drawings from three different designers. Ron likes one design, you like another. Every time you suggest a drawing, Ron disagrees. You feel like pulling out your hair or his, if he had enough of it. What do you do?

   a. You walk to the door and say, "Ron, you win. Pick whatever logo you like."

   b. You take a deep breath, sit down and smile at Ron. "Maybe we need another opinion," you suggest. "Let's ask someone objective to help us choose."

   c. You stack all the drawings and glare at Ron. "You are standing in the way of this company's progress."

4. You're the only woman manager in a group planning the annual report. Everyone wants each department highlighted. Your

colleagues are talking loudly, trading insults. No one is listening to anyone else. What do you do?

a. Allow the tension and conflict to get to you and leave the room.

b. Wave your arms and call for, "TIME OUT!" Once you have everyone's attention, ask them to sit down and say, "Let's brainstorm ways we can all benefit from the annual report."

c. Shout, "All you guys care about is numbers! *People* make this company and the sooner you realize that, the better."

5. You are in the middle of a presentation to Accounting, describing the new *Policy and Procedures* manual. While you talk, you notice your audience scribbling, running calculators and gazing out the window. How do you handle this?

a. Hurry through your presentation and slink out of the room as quickly as possible.

b. Take a brief break and think about what is going wrong. Get feedback from a couple of key people. Are you using language they care about? Are you emphasizing benefits they can relate to? Give your presentation a quick analysis and continue with increased eye contact and energy.

c. Plow through your speech and tell a friend later, "Just as I thought. Those accountants only care about their calculators."

SCORING
If you chose Bs for your answers, you have the sense of collaboration and empathy that marks a potentially great negotiator. If you chose As, you need to boost your self-esteem and ask more clearly for what you want. If you chose Cs, take a deep breath and consider the fine art of collaboration.

MEETINGS IN THE MIDDLE: SECRETS OF NEGOTIATION

Deirdre wants the company to sponsor a child care center. Each time she talks to her boss, Bob, he says, "Interesting idea. Let me consider it."

Deirdre feels Bob is not taking her suggestions seriously. Today, at her department's monthly meeting, she stands up and says to Bob, "I demand to hear your response to my suggestion for child care."

Bob taps his pen on his legal tablet and answers, "Deirdre, we just can't afford to open a child care center."

Deirdre feels Bob isn't taking her seriously. Why should he? His wife stays home with his kids. All he cares about is the bottom line. During the rest of the meeting, Deirdre's fuming. She vows, "I'm going to get this company to create a child care center no matter what."

After the meeting, Rose, Bob's secretary, draws Deirdre aside and says, "Deirdre, if you'd bring Bob some numbers on that child care center, I bet he'll give it serious thought."

"He'll never approve the idea," Deirdre says and stomps back to her office.

REASONABLE PEOPLE WHO ARE EQUALLY INFORMED SELDOM DISAGREE.

Fast Fact

Learn the universal law of negotiations: Work toward an agreement, not toward a victory.

Action

Deirdre presented her demands as the only solution to the problem of child care for employees. She can present a list of alternatives and a list of ways corporate day care will benefit the company. She can create her lists by considering, "What do Bob and I agree about?"

- Find an area of common ground. In Deirdre's situation, both she and Bob want the employees to be happy and productive. Both want to cut down on absenteeism. Using these common areas, Deirdre can work toward a proposal that meets her need for company-supported child care and Bob's need to keep down expenses.

- Be prepared to accept change when you negotiate. Negotiation is a series of informed compromises.

- Be clear about what you want. Know your own value system. Know what you can give up and where you draw the line.

THE DREAM TEAM: HOW BEING A TEAM PLAYER STRENGTHENS YOUR NEGOTIATING SKILLS

Deirdre can't give up the idea of day care. She's angry at Bob and furious with herself for not being more prepared to debate the issue with him. She wishes she didn't get upset so easily. Her first impulse is to pack her belongings, grab her briefcase, and go home.

MOST WOMEN HAVE EXPERIENCE WITH COOPERATIVE PLAY RATHER THAN STRUCTURED TEAM PLAY.

Fast Fact

As children, women's play doesn't necessitate problem solving and agreement reaching. Their play is based on liking a select few companions. Therefore, women are often unprepared for the structured team approach and natural conflict of the typical workplace.

Action

If Deirdre considers the problem from Bob's viewpoint, she will feel the pressure of bottom-line performance and understand his objections. Thus, she understands his perspective and strengthens her own negotiating skills.

She needs to think of a team or win/win approach, with day care as an end result. She needs to brainstorm for solutions that meet Bob's economic needs and the employees' needs for child care.

Most of you can identify with Deirdre's initial desire to remove herself from the stress, conflict and possible rejection. But confrontation and problems are a normal part of the business environment. Learn how to depersonalize the situation and calmly solve things.

COPING WITH CONFLICT: ARE YOU COOL OR DO YOU CRUMBLE?

Okay, so you have a conflict with your boss. How can you tell if you're taking things too personally? Watch out for these behaviors:

+ *Avoidance.* You pull back from her and avoid her whenever possible. You bury the problem and complain about it every chance you get.

- *Passive-aggressive behavior.* Instead of discussing your conflict with your boss, you make snide remarks about her to your co-workers. You see her working at her desk and you think, "I'll get you."

- *Undermining.* You poke holes in whatever she says. You look for the negative.

- *Fear.* If she looks good, you figure it hurts your chances of advancement. You withhold information. You don't realize when another woman succeeds, it enhances your chances of success.

POWER TOOLS FOR GETTING YOUR POINT ACROSS

Cynthia goes to the doctor about a persistent feeling of tiredness she'd experienced for months.

"It's just stress," her doctor contends. "It's normal for a person in your position."

Cynthia thinks, "I know there's more to it. I deserve treatment."

She also thinks, "But he's a doctor. He knows what he's talking about. I'll wait and see what happens."

Cynthia returns home feeling dismissed and defeated.

WOMEN'S INITIAL TENDENCY IS TO DEFER TO AUTHORITY.

Fast Fact

You give away personal power when you don't use your right to question authority. Know it is your right to be taken seriously.

Action

Don't be afraid to question authority. Be assertive and speak out.

What messages are you sending?

Don't say:

I don't know as much as he does.

I don't have the right to question him.

I feel inferior.

Nobody will listen.

It's not worth the work.

Do say:
> I know as much or more than he does.
> I have every right to ask questions.
> People are interested in what I have to say.
> I'm worth it.

Woman's Wisdom: The Female Advantage in Negotiating

Jackie developed a flex-time procedure that isn't working. People are coming in late and no one is really keeping track of their hours. Jackie's manager, Marie, suspects that many people are slacking off. Still, Jackie is passionate about flex-time. She thinks it's a working mother's right.

Marie says, "Jackie, I feel the current flex-time procedure is costing us a lot of money."

"But we need flex-time. Some people have already let their babysitters go. You can't let money get in the way of this!"

"I'm willing to experiment with the idea of flex-time for another month," Marie says. "But with the following modifications."

Marie suggests changes and Jackie listens carefully, then adds a few of her own. They both agree to try the new system for a month.

BECAUSE WOMEN DO NOT GENERALLY HAVE A COMPETITIVE MIND-SET, THEY BRING A WIN/WIN ATTITUDE TO BUSINESS PROBLEMS.

Fast Fact

Thinking cooperatively is a female advantage that supports you in difficult situations.

Action

Meet your needs without taking advantage of others. Don't worry about winning; find a solution that meets everyone's needs.

When Jackie sees problems from her boss's viewpoint, she will feel the pressure of bottom-line performance and understand Marie's objections.

Jackie might work with Marie to define the financial benefits that flex-time brings. Examples include:

- Increased productivity because of less tardiness and absenteeism.

- Reduced employee turnover and increased employee loyalty. All these have a positive impact on the company's profits.

By seeing Marie's viewpoint, Jackie invites Marie to do the same for her. She also better understands the boss's problems.

Having a cooperative win/win attitude is the foundation of effective negotiation. Take the initiative in understanding the other's point of view. He is more likely to see it your way.

You Have the Power: Nine Ways to Negotiating Know-How

Take your natural inclination to collaborate and add the answers to these six questions: *Who, When, Why, How, Where* and *What?* You'll have the ingredients for a powerful negotiating strategy.

WHO: KNOW YOUR DECISION MAKERS. Sometimes you think the decision makers are only managers or supervisors, those in obvious positional power. But other people often have real power in influencing the course of decision making.

Who is a well-hidden power player? Which associates, assistants, secretaries, and so on have large networking and personal influence? Get to know these people. Build strong relationships with them and they'll help support your position in negotiating.

WHEN: WATCH YOUR TIMING. "George, I need to talk to you," Fran says. She rehearsed her speech four times last night and she's bursting with energy. George sits at his desk, both hands around his coffee mug. He takes a sip when Fran walks in and looks at her.

"Let's talk after ten, Fran," he says.

"George, this idea will make your day. You will be so excited." She sits down across from him and spreads a huge smile.

"I'm anxious to hear it, but I focus much better after ten," George says. He finishes his coffee and pours more from the small coffee pot on his credenza.

"No, George, I won't be put off. I know how busy you get. Now listen carefully. . . ."

NOT PAYING ATTENTION TO A PERSON'S BIORHYTHM AND TIMING MAY COST YOU.

Fast Fact
Timing affects your listener's enthusiasm, energy and objectivity.

Action

Fran might say, "George, I have an idea I want to share with you. I need fifteen uninterrupted minutes. Is this afternoon a good time?"

This direct request gives George a chance to say, "This afternoon is hectic. What about tomorrow at 11:00?"

You know people who are bright and breezy first thing in the morning and other people who start picking up steam around early afternoon. Use this information to know the best time to approach people.

The day of the week also affects timing. Some managers are stressed out on Mondays, needing to get organized, to solve the problems of the weekend. Other managers get disinterested on Friday afternoons. Their minds are already on the weekend. Notice the days when your boss is most accessible and receptive. Find a stress-free place to talk to him: a conference room, somebody else's office or take him out to lunch.

Your manager isn't the only person with delicate timing. Know your own best times. Know what days of the week are best for you and what hours of the day. Know when you feel the most energy. You get your point across more effectively when you feel balanced and energetic.

If you have low energy and feel out of sorts, you tend to take disappointment and rejection more personally.

WHEN: TIME TO BE SEEN. "Great article in the newsletter about you, Ginnie," George says.

"It was nothing, really."

"I bet your manager is really pleased."

"He didn't mention anything," Ginnie says.

Ginnie's been written up in the company newsletter for the high morale in her department. She wonders if her manager actually read the article. She wants to discuss a flex-time proposal with her manager, but isn't sure the timing is right.

HIGH VISIBILITY IS AN IMPORTANT ASPECT OF GETTING WHAT YOU WANT.

Fast Fact

Ask for what you need when you have high visibility.

Action

Use the "Santa Claus" effect to your advantage. Here's how it works. If you ask Susie to draw a picture of Santa Claus in July, she'll scribble a stick figure with a beard and dash out to play. But if you invite Susie to draw Santa on December 1, she'll draw an elaborate man with a reindeer sleigh, she'll color in the background and discuss her art with you.

Celebrate your own visible "seasons." Use your sense of timing when negotiating and enhance your chances of being heard and taken seriously.

WHEN TO SPEAK OUT: ZIPPERS AND LIPPERS. Eda worked hard on the marketing plan for ZZ company. But when the time came to present the team's ideas to the client, Joe acted like every idea was his. Eda was furious but she didn't know what to do. She didn't want to cause friction in front of a client. She didn't want to seem like a tattletale.

BE PREPARED TO SPEAK UP AND DEFEND YOUR CONTRIBUTIONS TO PROJECTS.

Fast Fact

Women often share their wonderful ideas too openly. Watch out for unscrupulous co-workers who like to pirate ideas and cash in on them. Don't spill your wisdom until you have it documented, dated, and you can prove that it's your fine thinking.

Action

Take charge of making yourself look good to your boss. You can't rely on anyone else to adequately praise you.

Eda might say, "Joe's right. We all worked hard developing that idea. Our commitment to brainstorming as a team will give you the support and creativity you need for your projects."

WHY: FIND THE FACTS, WEED OUT THE EMOTIONS. Kayla's hurriedly checking in to catch a flight to Chicago, then another to Detroit. The agent at the ticket counter says, "The flight to Chicago is an hour late."

Kayla is panic-stricken. How can she connect with her Detroit flight? She'll be late for her meeting. She hates this incompetent airline. She feels flustered and upset.

"We've made arrangements for you to take another plane," the agent says, after checking the computer.

"What?" Kayla says. She's so flustered and wound up, worrying whether she can catch a train, change airlines, and so forth, that she doesn't hear the agent.

Here's another way the agent might approach things.

"You'll arrive in Chicago on time," she says. "We've made reservations for you on our flight #310, in that your originally-scheduled flight was delayed."

Kayla checks her luggage without concern. There's no problem. The agent has handled everything and Kayla has nothing to worry about.

PRESENT INFORMATION BY FOCUSING ON THE PRIMARY CONCERN OF THE OTHER PERSON AND AVOID A LOT OF EMOTIONAL UPSET.

Fast Fact

As you listen, be aware of facts and feelings. Acknowledge your feelings and the other person's feelings and keep your focus on the outcome.

Action

Notice how in the second scenario, the agent has taken the time to analyze the passenger's reaction in advance, understand her problems and solve them. This insight decreases potential misunderstanding and upset.

HOW: THINK SOLUTIONS. Clara can't believe how people abuse the supply room. She's seen co-workers carrying reams of paper home, using way too many pens. Some take company envelopes and use them to mail personal bills. As part of the accounting team, Clara knows how high the office supplies expense is. She bets half the cost is employee abuse.

BE A PROBLEM SOLVER, NOT JUST A PROBLEM IDENTIFIER.

Fast Fact

Anyone can identify a problem. A team player develops suggestions on how to solve the problem.

Action

Developing "what if" thinking skills helps you prevent problems. This establishes you as a problem solver.

Clara needs to design some solutions to the office supply problem. She can use "what if" thinking and ask, "what if we gave each department an allotment? What if we had an office supply clerk in charge of checking out supplies? What if departments got a reward for conserving office supplies?"

Know the difference between the root of the problems and the symptom. When you see a problem, have several solutions before you make suggestions to management.

It's important to make your boss look good. Ask these questions about your proposed solutions:

♦ Does it save time?

♦ Does it help the budget?

♦ Does it increase your boss's visibility?

♦ How does it benefit the boss? The company?

Learn how to prevent problems. Get good at knowledgeable anticipation or "what if" thinking.

What if the company downsized?

What if the work force changed to an all-female work force?

What if all decisions were made by committee?

HOW: TALK THEIR LANGUAGE. Sue works for a miserly boss. He carries in his trash from home and dumps it in the office dumpster, so he won't have to pay an extra trash hauling fee. He saves scraps of paper and takes them home for his daughter to draw on. He puts a note on the coffee pot, saying, "Please pour just half a cup."

Fast Fact

Your language reflects your work values.

Action

Observe the speaker's style and learn the language he appreciates. Listen with your eyes and ears.

Sue observes her boss. When she has something to ask of him, she defines it in terms of saving money. She doesn't use flowery or persuasive language.

She speaks precisely and to the point, ending with, "Look how much money this idea will save," then she backs it up with numbers.

WHAT: EXPLORE ALL SOLUTIONS. Helen and Arnold want to get away for a long-needed vacation. Helen wants to relax, go to the mountains, take books, walk and meditate. Arnold wants to go to New York, see plays every day, stoke his cultural palate and really cut loose.

"How can we have fun on a vacation if we can't even agree where we want to go?" Helen wonders.

BE CLEAR ABOUT WHAT YOU WANT. ASK FOR WHAT YOU WANT IN A VARIETY OF WAYS.

Fast Fact

Use the GASP factor. If they don't gasp when you tell what you want, you haven't asked for enough.

Action

Write down what you want and don't give it away. Know your parameters. Be sure you ask for enough. Talk to co-workers, mentors, other experts and make sure your parameters are strong and reasonable.

Helen and Arnold can work out their vacation by clarifying the end results first. Helen can say, "I want to relax, forget about work, not think about anything serious."

"Great," Arnold says, "because that's what I have in mind, too. I want a fun, mindless trip."

Identify mutual problems. Ask yourself, "How do we want this conversation to end? What's in it for both of us?" This allows you to develop a mutually beneficial area to work toward.

With Helen and Arnold, they might say, "I want this conversation to end with a vacation plan that we both like."

Now that they realize they both want the same thing, they can explore different options for each of them having the vacation they crave. Maybe they can spend three days in each place. Maybe they can stay in a resort area that's near a big city, so they can relax and meditate part of the day and be wild and crazy in the city the other part.

WHERE: KEEP YOUR FOCUS ON THE BIG PICTURE. Susie wants to manage the big seminar her department is sponsoring. Her supervisor, Juan, doesn't think she has enough experience.

"Things go wrong at seminars," Juan says, "and I don't know that you can handle these situations."

"Last week when you were out of town, I handled several crises," Susie says.

"I don't feel comfortable dumping so much responsibility on you," Juan says. "But I might consider letting you work with Delores on this."

Susie leaves Juan's office feeling angry. She doesn't like Delores. Delores would nag and pick at her. They could never get along. Susie wants to be involved with the seminar but working with Delores sounds terrible.

CONCENTRATE ON THE WHOLE PICTURE, RATHER THAN DETAILS.

Fast Fact
Look beyond the "NOW" and think about outcome. When negotiating, the whole picture helps you see what you want.

Action
Susie can be involved in the seminar by letting go of her irritation toward Juan and Delores. By concentrating on her goal, she won't get overwhelmed by all she has to go through to be involved in the seminar. The energy in negotiation comes from the successful outcome.

GETTING YOUR OWN "SWEET" WAY: CONVINCING ADVERSARIES

Lena and Allen are stuck on how to proceed with the Summerson project.

"We need to develop a public relations strategy," Lena says.

"That won't solve the issue of personnel turnover," Allen says. "We need to do an employee survey."

Lena shakes her head. They've been talking for an hour and they haven't gotten anywhere.

ALWAYS START WITH POINTS OF AGREEMENT.

Fast Fact
Use the company mission statement as a point of reference. If you feel at odds about everything, say, "Would you agree that there's nothing we can agree on?"

Action

Clarifying the desired outcome can also serve as a point of agreement.

If you can't get what you want, don't be afraid to compromise and trade. For example, Beni wants a substantial raise. Her boss considered the matter and offered her $1000 less than she asked for.

"I'll take $1000 less," Beni says, "if you give me the equivalent in comp time, vacation days and training."

Know all the things you can ask for. If it's a salary negotiation, consider asking for flex-time, a computer terminal in your home, extra training, additional benefits, vacation days, and so forth.

Rule 1: Keep Focused

Ask your adversary to focus only on this problem.

Set time limits for one person talking and the other listening. Before you trade roles, have the listener paraphrase the talker's words.

"Did I capture what you were saying?" Eleanor asks.

"Well, I didn't really mean the part about the old ghosts scaring everyone to death," says Rodney.

The same dynamics work for more than one person:

+ Clarify the outcome.

+ Understand the points of agreement.

+ Discuss the ground rules.

+ Focus, paraphrase, timing.

Rule 2: Go for the Close

Women are often shy about bringing a negotiating session to a close. Ask for what you want. Say, "What will it take to close this deal?"

Or, try an assumptive close. If you've agreed that the company will offer a flex-time program in the next two months, say, "I'll expect those flex procedures from you by the end of next week."

Rule 3: Ask for Help When You Need It

Sometimes you need a third party, an objective listener to help you sort things out and offer insights that you haven't considered.

Asking for this objective help is hard for many women. As a woman, you've been expected to be a mediator and you've done it well. You may feel a sense of failure if you need someone to mediate for you. Remember, asking for help simply means getting assistance in removing road blocks and clarifying the end result. When you fear getting help and you are inflexible and controlling, you alienate people.

How Convincing Are You?

Test your new collaboration skills and evaluate how you have increased your negotiating prowess.

1. You proposed a new way of marketing your company's service. Your boss, Daryl, who has had your proposal for several weeks, finally calls you into his office. "This proposal definitely has merit. But it's just not economically feasible," he says. How do you respond?

   a. You lower your eyes and say quietly, "Thanks for considering it."

   b. You say, "That proposal describes just one of many ways we could revitalize marketing. I have other ideas I'd like to tell you about."

   c. "You don't fully understand the depth of that marketing proposal. I have considered every aspect. In the long run, that marketing plan will make us a lot of money."

2. Employee morale is low in your company. You want your boss to give the employees a party and authorize a casual dress day once a week. You're making notes, trying to think of the right time and way to approach him. His secretary comes into your office and says, "What are you working on so diligently?" You say:

   a. "Nothing important."

   b. You tell her about your project and ask her advice.

c. You cover your papers with both hands and say, "It's top secret."

3. For two hours you and your co-worker Ron have been trying to choose a new company logo. You have 20 drawings from three different designers. Ron likes one design, you like another. Every time you suggest a drawing, Ron disagrees. You feel like pulling out your hair or his, if he had enough of it. What do you do?

   a. You walk to the door and say, "Ron, you win. Pick whatever logo you like."

   b. You take a deep breath, sit down and smile at Ron. "Maybe we need another opinion," you suggest. "Let's ask someone objective to help us choose."

   c. You stack all the drawings and glare at Ron. "You are standing in the way of this company's progress."

4. You're the only woman manager in a group planning the annual report. Everyone wants each department highlighted. Your colleagues are talking loudly, trading insults. No one is listening to anyone else. What do you do?

   a. Allow the tension and conflict to get to you and leave the room.

   b. Wave your arms and call for, "TIME OUT!" Once you have everyone's attention, ask them to sit down and say, "Let's brainstorm ways we can all benefit from the annual report."

   c. Shout, "All you guys care about is numbers! People make this company and the sooner you realize that, the better."

5. You are in the middle of a presentation to Accounting, describing the new *Policy and Procedures* manual. While you talk, you notice your audience scribbling, running calculators and gazing out the window. How do you handle this?

   a. Hurry through your presentation and slink out of the room as quickly as possible.

   b. Take a brief break and think about what is going wrong. Get feedback from a couple of key people. Are you using language they care about? Are you emphasizing benefits they can relate to? Give your presentation a quick analysis and continue with increased eye contact and energy.

c. Plow through your speech and tell a friend later, "Just as I thought. Those accountants only care about their calculators."

GRAND TOTALS

Now you can get what you want with style, grace and ease. You have the negotiating skills to maneuver in the business world. This chapter has increased your knowledge of collaboration, your listening skills and your ability to hear and respond to information without personalizing it.

+ You know that negotiating requires change and collaboration.

+ You know how to judge another person's needs and how to speak to him or her in a persuasive and meaningful style.

+ You can singlehandedly handle a negotiating situation and you can also ask for an objective third party when you're getting nowhere.

+ You realize that timing, friendly language and benefit-orientation help you present your ideas in the best possible way.

+ You pay attention to people who support management as well as management. You realize the power of support staff and other associates and the importance of building strong relationships with them.

+ You ask clearly for what you want. You ask again if you're not heard the first time.

+ You make yourself visible through your problem-solving skills.

+ You practice "What if" thinking. For any problem, you have several solutions.

CAPTURING WHAT YOU'VE LEARNED

Things I've learned

_____

_____

Concepts I want to try

_____

_____

Great ideas I want to share with others

_____

_____

Things I want to know more about

_____

_____

Chapter Seven

◇

LISTENING: HOW TO MASTER THE MOST POWERFUL COMMUNICATION SKILL OF ALL

GOOD LISTENING SKILLS EQUAL GOOD PEOPLE SKILLS: TEST YOUR ABILITY

Listening is the difference between having or not having good people skills. You're a better everything when you listen. Use your people skills and determine how your good listening makes these scenes successful.

1. You walk into the lounge and everyone seems to be ignoring Marge prattle on about the computer network and how it's going to be on the fritz for the next three days. As she talks, she reaches down the front of her dress and pulls her bra strap back onto her shoulder, then stands in front of the coffee machine, blocking you from your morning fix. What do you do?

a. Look at the others over the rim of your glasses, roll your eyes and see if anyone else shares your opinion that Marge has crossed the threshold of insanity.

b. Say, "Marge, on your lunch break, you have got to check out the blue light special in lingerie."

c. Acknowledge to yourself, "For sure, Marge is weird and she's standing between me and my coffee. But what she's saying will affect my productivity this week." You mentally block out her annoying mannerisms and focus on what she's saying.

2. You're at the company's annual conference, and you're sitting three rows behind the podium. The speaker talks very fast as he addresses issues critical to your department. You're furiously taking notes, but you can't keep up with the volume of information. What do you do?

a. You think this is useless and a waste of your time. How does anyone in the company expect you to get this stuff when the speaker's talking like that?

b. You listen and write as fast as you can. There's no way you can keep up, so you look around and find a co-worker whose notes you can borrow when the pitiful presentation is over. You daydream about the mountain village you visited last spring and start making plans to return.

c. You listen for the main points and jot down key words. When you hear important information, you interrupt and say, "I didn't get that last point. Would you repeat that information?"

3. You've gathered several people together into the conference room for a scheduled training session. The consultant makes her opening remarks just as the window washers squeegee their way up to your floor. What do you do?

a. Watch the window washers. How many times does a man climb twenty stories to clean a woman's windows? Could be actors on a movie set for all you know. Your big break is just a pane away.

b. Take notes, listen to the squeegee, but alternate your concentration with the consultant. After all, she's expensive and it's coming out of your department's budget.

c. Say, "If you'll give me a moment, I can clear this up." Call Maintenance. If they can't move the window washers, then relocate to another room.

4. You played too hard last night. Today your stomach is a bit queasy, your back hurts and you want to go home. The company's best vendor will be here any minute. You're not sure if you can use her services, but you agreed to see her. Your secretary pokes her head in and announces the vendor has arrived. What do you do?

a. Invite the woman to come in. She begins her presentation. You hear what she's saying, but you are so preoccupied with your queasiness, you can't listen to anything she says.

b. Invite her in. You aren't sure you can use her services or if you have the budget. She's here, so you might as well let her go through the motions. You look at your watch, and wonder when she'll finish.

c. You acknowledge that you are not at your best and your ability to listen is impaired. You invite her in. Say, "I'd like to listen to your presentation, and now is not a good time. Could we take a look at our calendars and reschedule this meeting?" You are also up front with her and let her know you need to take a close look at how her services fit your needs at this time.

5. David, your boss, is furious. He flies into your office and plunks a box full of green pens on your desk. "You never get the order straight. Every time I let you requisition office supplies, you mess things up." What do you do?

a. Open the box. Examine the pens while he's yelling. Sure enough, they're all green. You check every box. Suppose Red Cross could use green pens?

b. Say, "Yeah, well, a little color in here may be nice. At least they're not bright red. Reminds me of Irene Behrends, my eighth grade English teacher."

    c. Say, "Let me repeat what you said. Every time I requisition office supplies, I mess things up."

6. Two months ago, you assigned a task force to study your company's long-distance telephone calls. You need to decide whether it would be to the company's advantage to get several 800 numbers. You expect them to come back with an affirmative answer. During their report, one member says, "Our company will be ready for an 800 number in six to eight months." What do you do?

    a. Go through your files. Try to figure out where they went wrong. Look at the ceiling. How could they be so misguided? Ask yourself why you hired them.

    b. Say, "Then, let's line it up right now. Beth, call the phone company. Tell them to hook us up."

    c. Say, "Six to eight months? That wasn't the answer I was expecting to hear. Tell me about your study and how you came to your conclusions."

7. You're an elementary school teacher. Your students finished a unit on space flight and one of them invites his uncle, a pilot, to come into the class and talk about piloting adventures. The uncle comes just before recess and he speaks in pilot jargon. What do you do?

    a. Say, "Thank you for coming. We're about ready for recess. You know kids. Can't keep them from having a little fun."

    b. Tell the kids to be polite and listen. Close the door. Pace up and down the aisles. Tap anyone who looks out the window. Sit at your desk. Cross out your guest speaker for next week and rewrite your lesson plans.

    c. Say, "I'm not sure we all know about 'vertical speed indicators.' Would you explain that?" Ask leading questions that you know will interest your students. Tell the students they'll get an extra ten minutes of recess after the adventure stories.

8. For years you worked in the machine shop. When you asked for a relocation into the offices, you were promoted to assistant

manager. You work with Chuck, a wonderful, nice-looking young man. Sometimes he mumbles and he's hard to understand, but then that adorable blonde in word processing seems to hear him very well. Is it him, or do you have a hearing loss? What should you do?

   a. Ignore him. Sooner or later he'll learn how to speak plainly if he wants to stay in management. It's not your problem. Don't jeopardize your future by pointing out a weakness in a man.

   b. Say, "What is it about you, Chuck? You talk like a teenager, all vowels, no consonants. How am I supposed to understand you?"

   c. You get into a habit of paraphrasing what Chuck says, ensuring you've understood him, and you also say, "Chuck, when I listen to you, I think I might be missing something important. You could help me if you'd slow down some and speak a little louder."

9. You're working with top people in the company putting together a total quality management conference. When the conference is nearly planned, your boss wants you to add Dennis to your committee. In your opinion, Dennis throws negative energy into the group. During a meeting when the team is scheduling events and lining up speakers, Dennis asks, "Who's running the numbers on this? Has anyone thought to clear them through me?" What do you do?

   a. Stand up and walk away from Dennis. Pour yourself a cup of coffee. You are totally convinced he has nothing important to add to this group. Tune him out.

   b. Say, "Way to concentrate, Dennis. The numbers are in Ted's office, already approved. If you don't mind. . . ."

   c. Recognize that Dennis is probably an obsessive F on the SELF profile, and that might be why your boss wants him on the team. Say, "I have a copy of the budget right here. Ted's approved the numbers. It would be helpful if you'd take a close look at it to see if there's something we've overlooked."

10. You are sorting the laundry when your 15-year-old comes in and says, "Social Studies is a total waste of my time. I hate the teacher. We haven't talked about one relevant thing yet. Six weeks I've been in this class and I'm sick of it. I want to drop it from my schedule." What do you do?

   a. You continue sorting socks and think to yourself, "This kid has a crisis a day." You ignore what she's saying. Tell her to run upstairs and bring down the laundry. You have no time to waste today.

   b. Say, "What do you mean, 'drop out'? Do you know how important that class is to your education? You can't expect everything in life to be fun and to your liking. Just buckle down and study. You can do it."

   c. You are concerned about your daughter's problem. You want to get to the bottom of this issue and you realize she'll need to do that at her own pace and time. You try to understand her. Right now, it's more important to listen with your eyes and heart than with your ears. You give her the space she needs by simply repeating for understanding. You say, "You're telling me Social Studies is a real pain and a waste of time."

SCORING

If you scored mostly As, you are taking little or no responsibility as a listener to connect with the speaker. You've become indifferent, and say to yourself, "If they can't communicate better than that, why should I try?"

If you scored mostly Bs, you are easily distracted, and you allow mannerisms, speakers' speech habits, visual distractions, fatigue or physical pain to break down the listening process.

If you scored all Cs, you are a great listener. You assume your share of responsibility for communication to happen. You are an active, empathic listener.

WHY WOMEN MAKE BETTER LISTENERS

Before the furniture company downsized, Jonathan had an administrative assistant, Marissa, who took notes for him at every important meeting. When the company reorganized, Marissa was promoted to manager of Retail Development. Much as he hated to see her move into another department, Jonathan encouraged Marissa to take the position.

This morning, Jonathan and Marissa are attending a presentation from a new East Coast vendor. To Marissa, the speaker is obviously stressed. He squeezes his face when Jonathan asks a question, and acts like Jonathan's questions are a direct threat. The materials are obviously high quality, but the speaker is terribly distracting.

When the presentation is over, Jonathan says, "We are not using that company. I'm sorry I dragged you through that."

"He certainly had distracting behavior," Marissa says, "but did you notice the quality of the lines of furniture he carries? And his prices are much lower than we've been paying."

"I didn't see that," Jonathan says. "When did he show us his price list?"

BAD LISTENERS HEAR WHAT THEY WANT TO HEAR. GOOD LISTENERS HEAR WHAT IS BEING SAID AND MEANT.

Fast Facts

Most workers spend about half of their business hours listening. The average listener has a 25% level of efficiency.

Action

You're a better everything when you listen. Listening is the difference between having or not having good people skills.

When people describe a good listener, they use words like "Patient, Open-minded, Sincere, Considerate, Focused." When the same people describe poor listeners, they use words like, "Self-Centered, Apathetic, Intolerant, Stubborn, Closed-minded."

Women usually make better listeners. Here's why.

- You're intuitive. You read between the lines, as if you can say back to the speaker, "I hear what you are not saying."
- You pick up on body language and trust it.

◆ You are less likely to attach your ego to the message. You're willing to get out of your place and see the message from another point of view.

HOW TO STOP CARRYING OLD BAGGAGE

When Nancy's company relocated her to Philadelphia, she thought the only visible baggage she carried with her was her personal belongings. Although she listens attentively to co-workers, sometimes she feels she's not worth listening to when she talks to supervisors, and that influences how she listens. Nancy wants to be forthright and open with Elaine, her boss. She doesn't want to appear intimidated, so she invites Elaine to lunch.

"I'd like some advice," Nancy begins.

Elaine puts down her fork. "What can I do for you?" she asks.

"I feel that something gets in my way when I'm listening to you, or to other superiors. I can't figure it out."

Elaine asks a few questions, then finally smiles, understanding. "You know women carry plenty of baggage from childhood. When we're young and easily influenced, we hear things like 'you're too young to understand' or 'don't argue with me.' You've got to let those clichés go."

CHILDHOOD MESSAGES INFLUENCE THE WAY YOU LISTEN TODAY.

Fast Fact
Your background creates certain filters. Awareness of these filters is the first step to overcoming them.

Action
Quickly, write down several keep-quiet clichés you heard as a child. Here are a few to get you started:

"Don't interrupt your elders."

"Don't argue with me."

"Be quiet and listen."

"Look at me when I talk to you."

"Don't speak until you are spoken to."

Take a close look at these. Do any of these old messages keep you from listening effectively, especially to people in authority?

Now you can develop new attitudes that support good listening with co-workers and supervisors. Select one or more affirmations from the following that will help you get rid of old baggage.

♦ I can only change myself. I don't have the power to change others.
♦ I accept others the way they are. They are my equals.
♦ Hearing people out without judging them helps me listen to them.
♦ I first seek to understand, then to be understood.

SELF-ASSESSMENT: HOW TO PERSONALIZE LISTENING

How well do you listen? Are you attending to the speaker? Do you process the message? If co-workers were asked to describe you as a listener, what words would they use?

Take this listening analysis and determine your strengths in listening skills. If you identify a weakness, this self-test will show you how to enhance your listening skills.

	Almost Never	Sometimes	Often	Almost Always
I define the purpose for listening.				
1. When someone is talking, I ask myself, "Why am I listening?"				
2. I ask myself, "Why is it important to listen to this person?"				
I listen fully to the speaker.				
3. I concentrate on the speaker, even if I am not interested.				

	Almost Never	Sometimes	Often	Almost Always

4. I concentrate on the speaker's message, even if I don't like his or her looks or voice tone.

5. I listen to the speaker without judging or criticizing.

6. I close out extraneous sounds so that I won't be distracted by them.

7. I ignore my personal problems as I listen.

8. I don't interrupt until the speaker is finished.

9. I use verbal and/or non-verbal messages to let the speaker know he or she has my full attention.

10. I take notes to help me understand and remember.

I can process the message.

11. I listen for cues that tell me what the speaker is feeling (uncertain, worried, angry).

12. I try to put myself in the speaker's place.

13. I recognize words have different meanings to different people.

14. I think about the speaker's message, and what additional information I need to know.

	Almost Never	Sometimes	Often	Almost Always

I can form a response.

15. I restate the message to confirm my understanding.

16. I probe for additional information.

17. I evaluate how well I am listening based on the other person's reaction to my responses.

A Personal Analysis:

Three of my strongest listening qualities are:

1) _____

2) _____

3) _____

Two things people say about me as a listener are:

1) _____

2) _____

If there's one thing that gets in the way of my listening, it is:

_____

Three areas where I could improve my listening skills are:

1) _____

2) _____

3) _____

HOW TO MAKE THE COMMUNICATION PROCESS WORK FOR YOU

As a regional manager, Laurie spends nearly 75 percent of her time on concentrated listening and she tires easily. When she's on the telephone, her energy level picks up. When the pace slows, her energy level drops. She mentioned her high energy/low energy fluctuation to her doctor.

"A good listener burns energy when she listens," her doctor tells her. "Your heart rate speeds up, your blood circulates faster, and your temperature goes up. You spend so much time listening."

WHEN YOU ARE SPEAKING OR LISTENING, ASSUME 51% OF THE RESPONSIBILITY FOR COMMUNICATION.

Fast Fact

People spend more time listening than any other communication activity. The communication process looks like this: 40% listening, 35% talking, 16% reading, 9% writing.

Action

The communication process begins by knowing the difference between hearing and listening.

Hearing is a passive activity. You're not actively involved, you're simply allowing sound waves to penetrate your ears. When you're listening, you are an active participant determining the meaning of what you hear. You can probably recall a time when you heard, but did not listen. This occurs frequently at night. Have you ever awakened suddenly, and wondered if that was really a sound, or was it just your imagination?

When you're communicating, you're involved in a four-step communication loop.

Step 1   The speaker sends a message.

Step 2   The listener hears the message.

Step 3   The listener converts the message into a personal code and determines what the speaker is saying.

Step 4   The listener responds to the speaker. Both listener and speaker respond with verbal and nonverbal reactions.

Who's responsible for communication, the speaker or the listener?

Seventy percent believe the speaker is responsible. People with strong listening skills assume more than half of the responsibility for communication. The effective listener listens beyond the words. Listen with your ears and your eyes. Watch for a cluster of nonverbal clues. Your eyes are your greatest listening instrument. When nonverbal clues contradict verbal, trust the nonverbal.

For example, when you talk to Mary and she looks at her watch, it's possible she's curious about the time. However, you'll receive a strong suggestion that she's not interested in the conversation if she looks at her watch, taps a pen and begins to lean away.

As a listener, you control the communication process. Body language, such as direct eye contact, asking questions, and showing interest, keeps the speaker focused on the message.

An experiment conducted at a university revealed the effects of how much control the listener had on the speaker.

A group of students were brought into an auditorium to listen to a presentation. During the first section, the audience showed no interest. Everyone slumped in their chairs, read books and fumbled through personal belongings. At a prearranged signal, they all sat up and paid attention.

A videotape revealed the speaker was nourished by the audience's attention. He became more animated and interacted strongly with the students.*

In another experiment, a researcher asked a group of participants which among the following situations would be the worst:

A listener negates everything you say.

A listener is indifferent to what you say.

The majority of the participants said they'd prefer indifference to negativism.

The researcher then invited the participants to test their theory. In the experiment, each person revealed a special project three times to a listener. The first time, the listener responded by affirming the project. "I think it's a great idea. I know it will work. I'm sure you're the person who can make it happen."

The second time, the listener responded negatively. "That will never work. It's a corny idea. We've been through this before. It didn't work then, and it won't work now."

The third time, the listener looked away, picked a fingernail, looked down at the floor, rolled her eyes in boredom.

"Indifference is the worst," one woman reported. "Even with negative comments, there's still an exchange of energy."

As an active listener, you prevent the breakdown of communication. Your listening skills encourage the speaker to share the information you need to do your work, and they make you a leader in the communication team.

* Excerpted from National Press Publications, Inc. *The Power of Effective Listening*, a division of National Seminars Group. National Press Publications Inc.

Good Listening Puts You in Control

As a graphics designer, Nikki is constantly reading and decoding messages from business clients. Most of her clients can see the image they want in their minds, but they struggle to describe the image in words.

According to Nikki, the most dreaded seven words in the design industry are, "I'll know it when I see it." As a designer, she can't afford to rack up hours in trial and error graphics. From the initial meeting, Nikki uses her eyes and ears to balance her analytical and creative skills.

She "listens" to the client's hands, posture, vocabulary, dress code, sometimes even the office decorations.

GOOD LISTENERS LISTEN WITH A PURPOSE.

Fast Fact

The listening process begins when you define your purpose for listening.

Action

Ask yourself, "If I listen carefully, what can I get out of this?" Then ask, "What will I accomplish by listening?" When you know why you're concentrating, you'll focus your listening energy.

Make sure you are physically attending to the message.

+ *Maintain eye contact about 60 percent of the time.*

+ *Adjust your body posture.* Be relaxed and alert at the same time. Lean forward when you think the speaker is giving you important information, or when you want the speaker to know you're concentrating on the message.

+ *Provide verbal and/or nonverbal acknowledgment.* Nod your head. Use your eyebrows to express concern, relief, joy, enthusiasm. Smile, if appropriate. Take notes. Use open body language when you need the speaker to know you're open to the conversation.

+ *Clear your mind.* Do this before you enter the meeting or before the conversation. Jot down a few questions you want the speaker to discuss. Give yourself a block of time for the conversation. If you think other ideas will scramble for your attention, say to the speaker, "I want to give you my attention for a full 30 minutes. Please ask your assistant to interrupt us at 10:30. That way, I won't have to be constantly checking my watch."

• *Avoid distracting behaviors.* Sometimes the speaker's behavior interferes with your listening efforts. He might take his glasses on and off, or squirm in his chair. He could have an eye twitch. Have you ever noticed how many times the speaker connects sentences with "... and ..."? What about speakers who say, "you know," or "like, you know what I mean?" Acknowledge to yourself, "I find this behavior distracting," then shut it off. Be clear about your purpose for listening. Block out the annoying mannerisms; then you can maintain focus.

You've defined your purpose, attended to the message, and as you listen, you are processing the message.

Imagine you are a pilot trying to land a 747 at a huge international airport where a flight takes off and lands every 30 seconds. The first time you receive information, or in this analogy, the first time you land, you take in different levels of data. What's the flight pattern? Which runway do I land on? Who's affected by the decision to land? What stands in my way? Which crossroads will I take to the disembarking gate?

When you're listening to new information, your brain creates a similar strategy. Your senses pick up information on radar, then they act like traffic control giving your brain directions on where the information should land. The brain passes information from one cell to the next and creates a landing pattern. The first time information lands, it feels awkward and "foreign." Each time you hear the information, the cell pattern (or flight pattern) gets shorter.

The first time you drove to a friend's house, you asked for directions, read street signs, looked for landmarks, and felt relieved when the directions actually worked. Now you can almost put the car on autopilot because your mind has processed the directions so many times. Your brain created a short cut.

When it's time for you to call upon the processed information, you retrieve it in the same way the brain stored it.

Have you ever dialed a telephone number so many times that you could punch the numbers automatically on the telephone pad? What happens when you need an operator's assistance?

Since your brain processed the information using a visual path, you'll have to recall the number visually before you can verbally give it to her.

If you've learned something through listening, your brain searches the auditory path. When you are actively listening, information gets stored on both sides of the brain in milliseconds. One side of the brain assigns pictures to the words you're hearing, another side analyzes the information and gives it meaning. Back to side one to put information in sequence, zap across to side two to make the parts fit together to form the whole picture.

All of this happens automatically. When you mentally depart from a conversation, you feel like the information is getting jumbled. The path gets unfocused and the brain must begin processing again.

You can process a maximum amount of information when you use more than one sense at a time.

For example, if you're listening to something difficult, and you eat apple slices or pineapple chunks at the same time, you're combining two senses to make the listening and decoding process more efficient. Plus, you'll have better concentration. Since active listening burns energy, you're replacing the burned calories with complex carbohydrates.

The nation's best brainstorming consultants serve high energy foods during the work sessions. If you're involved in a brainstorming session, you'll burn more calories than if you were swimming because you're actively listening and attending to the message while your brain is processing. This gives you sustained energy to respond to the speaker.

Responding is the fourth phase of the listening process.

How to Use the SELF Profile to Increase Your Listening Effectiveness

Last month, Julia, an officer in the X-Rae Corporation, analyzed the quality of letters going out from her office. She knows the company is losing clients over lazy writing and poor editing and decided to bring in an executive writing consultant. Julia wants people in several departments to buy into training sessions. She put together an ad hoc committee of managers to help determine how X-Rae can make the most of their consultant's time.

As they begin meeting, Julia knows she'll have to be a skillful listener. Not only to the words, but to the actions of each manager.

Elizabeth brings pretzels and mozzarella sticks to the meeting. "Who needs a letter when you can give parties? That puts us in direct contact with our clients. No one has time to read, anyway."

Jerome folds his arms across his chest. "Show me how the consultant is going to save clients. If the client leaves because of a little bad grammar, they were looking for a reason to leave, anyway."

Bonita sharpens her pencil, then returns to the table. "What's the consultant's fee? Whose budget does it come from? And wouldn't we save money if we just bought a dozen dictionaries?"

Lenore reaches across the table and places her hands over Bonita's. "Communication is more than a crisp dictionary of words. It's the tone, the friendly style, the look of the letter. A consultant helps us connect with the reader."

As Julia listens, she knows each person made an important point. To be an effective listener, she needs to acknowledge why they said what they did.

KNOW THE FORCES THAT DRIVE YOU AND OTHERS.

Fast Fact
Each person has a specific force which drives them to listen and respond in a certain way.

Action
Continuously refer to the SELF Profile as you evaluate and build your listening skills. Each person on Julia's committee is making an important point and it's Julia's job to know what motivates them to say what they do.

Elizabeth is an S. She wants to make the meeting fun. She sees the training session as an opportunity to get together with friends, get away from the phones and work with colleagues to hone an important skill.

Jerome is an E. He wants to know the bottom line. What's the point of the meeting? What's the point of the training session? Julia knows all participants will eventually ask, "What's the point?" It just happens to be on Jerome's front lobe.

Lenore is an L. She wants everyone to get along, and that includes getting along with the consultant, committee members and the clients. In Lenore's mind, getting along is how X-Rae keeps customers.

Bonita is an F. She's a 'show me the facts' communicator. While a dictionary is certainly an important tool in written communication, Julia knows written communication goes way beyond the nuts and bolts of definitions. If she intends to involve the Financial and Technical departments in this training, she has to appeal to their fact-centered personalities.

Julia well understands the advantages of listening to all participants. As she and the consultant design the seminar, Julia needs to understand that each manager listens and looks for what motivates her. Julia's effectiveness will increase significantly when she keeps this in mind as she moves them to work for the good of the entire group.

Three Ways to Make Your Response Show You Care

As a middle manager for a computer company, Tillie has to listen to people at both ends of the management structure. In order to stay ahead of business and retail computer demands, the company has decided to reorganize. No one will lose their job. In fact, several people will receive promotions, salary increases and improved benefits. Some people will be asked to relocate.

Reorganization will mean upheaval for some, rewards for others. Tillie must listen to upper and lower management so that she can keep her department flowing smoothly during the transitional period.

Tillie makes sure she asks plenty of probing questions.

THE GOAL OF PROBING IS TO DRAW PEOPLE OUT TO SHOW YOU CARE.

Fast Fact
Your response tells the speaker you know why you're listening, you're attending to the message and you're processing the information.

Action
Here are some ways to respond.

1. **Paraphrase.** Begin your response by paraphrasing the speaker's message. This helps you "check out" the information, and at the same time helps you through the processing stage.

Therapists use this technique in couples counselling. Before the next spouse speaks, the therapist asks the listener to clarify or paraphrase the message given.

2. **Repeat.** Use repeat strategy for two reasons.

    a. *Repeat details when you need to be specific.* "We're relocating twenty-two employees and no one will lose their job. Is that correct?"

    b. *Repeat a statement if you think the speaker is using judgmental, critical, angry, or global language.* When you repeat, the speaker hears what is said. You repeat, or reflect back a mirror image of what was said. Suppose your boss says, "Ellen, you always mess up when you work on this." Then you repeat the statement, "You think I always mess up when I work on this." When you repeat, this helps the speaker understand the unfairness of the statement.

3. **Probe.** Ask as many questions as it takes to help you understand. Everyone gains when you probe. The speaker gains because you're showing your interest by asking more questions. You gain because you're refining and processing the message.

    You can use two types of questions when probing.

    a. *Closed-ended questions.* These need a one- or two-word response. Where are you going? Do you want some coffee? What year is that car? How old are you?

    b. *Open-ended questions.* These require thought. For example, "The McFay account is coming up for renewal. How do you think we should handle it?" Avoid questions that look for an agreement, such as, "Don't you think that. . . ." And avoid questions that make you sound demanding. "When are you going to do something about. . . ."

4. **Take an action.** As a result of listening, you move into action.

5. **Store information.** Think about it; mull it over.

6. **Choose to forget the information.**

REMOVING BARRIERS IMPROVES YOUR LISTENING SKILLS

Two days ago, Jack scheduled an appointment with Theresa. Theresa knows this is an important meeting, and she knows she needs to listen carefully to the research Jack has gathered.

When he arrives at her office, Theresa welcomes him, and then she calls her assistant. "Hold all my calls, will you?"

Although it seems like a small request to make, Jack immediately senses several things about Theresa. She's getting ready for his presentation, she's blocking out disruptions, and she's made him feel important.

Jack's respect for Theresa increases and he feels a greater sense of responsibility to deliver a meaningful presentation.

REVEAL YOUR PEOPLE SKILLS BY ELIMINATING LISTENING BARRIERS.

Fast Fact

The quality of the message is directly related to the barriers you remove.

Action

Recognize the barriers that interfere with your performance as a listener. Review the **Barrier at a Glance** chart to help you identify the most common distractions and interruptions.

When you face a distraction, acknowledge that it interferes with your listening. If it's within your power, eliminate the barrier.

Barriers can be physical, emotional or intellectual. A physical barrier can be something external or internal. Likewise, emotional and intellectual barriers can also come from inside or outside yourself. This chart gives you an example of internal and external barriers to listening.

BARRIER AT A GLANCE

External Barriers

Physical	*Emotional*	*Intellectual*
Noise	Indifference	Content is unfamiliar
Visual distractions	Target for speaker's emotions	Jargon or unfamiliar words
Climate: too hot or cold		
Speaking too loudly or too softly		

Internal Barriers

Physical	Emotional	Intellectual
Fatigue	Hearing what you want to hear	Doing two things at once
Pain	Personal problems	Difficulty remembering
Mental fatigue	Jumping to conclusions	Difficulty processing information
Hearing Loss	Reacting emotionally	
	Being biased	

How to Overcome the Barriers to Effective Listening

EXTERNAL PHYSICAL. External physical barriers may be the easiest to overcome because they are the easiest to spot, and you have the greatest control over them.

EXTERNAL EMOTIONAL. Are you indifferent? Check it out. Now may not be a good time to talk. You might be a target for the speaker's emotions and you need to manage your limits. Ask for two or three minutes of attention.

Say, "Bob, it's clear to me you feel angry about this situation and I feel blamed for this. I'm not willing to talk about it under these conditions. I'll talk about it later (this afternoon or tomorrow morning) when we can be rational about it."

EXTERNAL INTELLECTUAL. Don't assume the meaning is in the word. Meanings are in people, not in words. Ask for clarification. Slow the speaker, ask for additional information. Paraphrase the message to ensure you are on track.

INTERNAL PHYSICAL. If you are tired, physically, mentally, or both, you can't be at your best. Most of us can't push through the pain and exhaustion. Accept your body's message. Postpone and reschedule your important listening.

If you're having difficulty hearing, make an appointment with an audiologist. Hard as it may seem, you may also need to acknowledge the aging process and schedule fewer appointments, or give yourself quiet moments to regroup when you feel fatigued.

INTERNAL EMOTIONAL. What's the force that drives you to listen? Make it a practice to hear the person out before drawing a conclusion. Know what triggers your hot button. Sometimes a colloquialism will stop a conversation. Do you find yourself easily distracted by buzzwords, jargon, labels or clichés that cause you to shut down?

INTERNAL INTELLECTUAL. Most of us can't concentrate on two separate subjects at the same time. Prepare yourself intellectually to listen. Put mental distractions aside and focus on the present topic. Schedule time for listening.

If you'd like to improve your concentration and memory, invest in yourself. Sign up for classes that teach you how to absorb information. Becoming an effective listener is a skill-building process. It takes lots of practice.

HOW YOU LISTEN MAKES THE DIFFERENCE

Helen collects people. Co-workers from all over the company come to her because she practices active listening.

Martin leans over the top of her cubicle and tells her several people are way behind on budget projections. Helen forwards her telephone to voicemail and maintains eye contact while Martin talks. When he's finished, she asks him if he has a minute to review the final numbers on her budget.

An hour later, Julia steps into Helen's office, frantically waving a report she's typing for Helen. "This report is insane. I don't understand any of it."

"You don't understand any of it?" Helen repeats.

"Well, this whole third paragraph. It's filled with technical stuff."

"You're right, it's loaded with jargon. Let me explain it."

For ten minutes, Julia complains about her frustration with the company's internal language. Finally, Helen and Julia work together to "decode" the report. When they're finished, Helen says, "Thanks for asking questions. This is an important project to me."

CREATE AN ATTITUDE THAT SAYS YOU'LL SEEK FIRST TO UNDERSTAND. IN RETURN, PEOPLE WILL TRY TO UNDERSTAND YOU.

Fast Fact

Respond to the speaker's feelings and you'll get a clearer message of what she's trying to tell you.

Action

Respond to the speaker's feelings through observation, interpretation and verification.

"Observe" body language. Don't miss a thing. It all has a meaning.

"Interpret" nonverbal signals against the words. If they don't match, the truth is hiding behind nonverbals.

"Verify" what you're hearing. Ask questions. Check to make sure you're processing the message.

Empathic Listening: The Highest Form of Listening

Chloe zips around the house trying to get dinner on the table at the same time she mulls over an argument she had with a co-worker. Richie's watching cartoons and he needs to be at soccer practice at 7:00. Kristen is on the telephone making plans for the weekend and has theater rehearsal at 7:30. Mike, Chloe's husband, thinks he might have to work late, but it all depends on whether a client stays in town overnight.

Richie saunters into the kitchen. "My teacher thinks I cheated on my science test."

"What? Why would she say that?" Chloe asks. She opens a package of spaghetti noodles and tosses them into a pan of hot water.

"I don't think she likes me." Richie sits on the floor and pokes a toothpick into his tennis shoes.

Chloe stirs the hamburger. "Of course she likes you. What kind of a teacher makes her students think she doesn't like them?"

Richie coughs. "I think I'm getting the flu."

"What?" Chloe wonders what she'll do if Richie is home with the flu tomorrow and she needs to be at work to smooth relations with a co-worker.

Richie places his hands on his mother's cheeks, brings her face down to him and says, "Mom, please listen to me with your eyes."

LISTEN WITH EMPATHY AND YOU'LL UNDERSTAND THE FEELINGS AND ISSUES THAT REALLY MATTER.

Fast Fact

Empathy is a Greek word that means, "listening with the eyes and the heart."

Action

You can participate in listening on different levels. You might pretend to be listening, but your attention is elsewhere. Or you might select what you want to hear. As an attentive listener, you hear, but you may be missing the deeper issues. Empathic listening is the highest form of listening. You listen with your ears, eyes and heart. You understand the feelings and issues that really matter.

When you listen with empathy, you create a psychologically safe place for the speaker. Empathy is:

* Nonjudgmental.
* Noncritical.
* Nonthreatening.

Listen with your eyes and reflect feelings. You do not need to agree or accept the position of the other person. You simply reflect feelings, allowing the other person to get at the real issue at their own time and pace.

It sounds easy, but it's difficult to do. Few people have skill in empathic listening. You haven't been taught how or haven't had role models. Here's the kind of listening most experience:

Evaluation	Sizing up or down, approval and disapproval, agreeing or disagreeing
Tons of	You should . . . You shouldn't . . . You oughta . . .
Advice	You gotta . . . Next time you better . . .
Shrinking	You know what's wrong with you . . . The source of your problem is . . . What you need to do is . . .

Empathy does none of these. Empathy reflects feelings. Let's slip back into Chloe's kitchen and watch her listen empathetically to Richie.

PLAY IT AGAIN, CHLOE

Richie: My teacher thinks I cheated on my science test.

Chloe: That must make you sad.

Richie: Yeah. I don't think she likes me.

Chloe: You feel she's picking on you.

Richie: Yeah, she doesn't pick on any other kids.

Chloe: Doesn't feel fair, does it?

Richie: No, it's not fair at all. I don't feel good. I think I have the flu.

Chloe: Going to school tomorrow is the last thing you want to do.

Richie: Yeah, can I stay home?

Chloe: Staying home may solve the problem?

Richie: No, I guess not. I'd still have to take the stupid science test.

Chloe: I'd be happy to help you, if you want my help.

Notice that Chloe did not agree with Richie. By reflecting feelings she let him come around to the real problem.

You will not use empathic listening every time you listen. It's best to use when the speaker's message has strong emotional components. Become an empathic listener when you're not sure you understand the message, and when you suspect the speaker doesn't think you understand.

Give clues to indicate that you intend to be an empathic listener. Create a safe space physically and psychologically. Say things like, "Hold my calls." "Let me rearrange my schedule so that we can meet." "This sounds too important for a telephone visit. Meet me in the lounge in two minutes." "Do you mind if I close the door? I think we need some privacy."

Steven Covey says, "Empathic listening seeks first to understand, then to be understood."[*]

[*] Steven Covey. *The Seven Habits of Highly Effective People*, copyright 1989. Simon and Schuster.

When you seek to understand the speaker, you:

+ Reduce defensiveness.
+ Clarify values and end results.
+ Jointly develop another way to look at the problem that will meet the needs of both parties.

As an empathic listener, you listen at the deepest level. Your first priority is to understand. When you do so, your chances of being understood greatly increase.

How Well Do You Listen?

Read through these scenes again and notice the kinds of listening. Who's an active listener and who is an empathic one? What are the barriers to listening and how would you overcome them?

1. You walk into the lounge and everyone seems to be ignoring Marge prattle on about the computer network and how it's going to be on the fritz for the next three days. As she talks, she reaches down the front of her dress and pulls her bra strap back onto her shoulder, then stands in front of the coffee machine, blocking you from your morning fix. What do you do?

    a. Look at the others over the rim of your glasses, roll your eyes and see if anyone else shares your opinion that Marge has crossed the threshold of insanity.

    b Say, "Marge, on your lunch break, you have got to check out the blue light special in lingerie."

    c. Acknowledge to yourself, "For sure, Marge is weird and she's standing between me and my coffee. But what she's saying will affect my productivity this week." You mentally block out her annoying mannerisms and focus on what she's saying.

2. You're at the company's annual conference, and you're sitting three rows behind the podium. The speaker talks very fast as he addresses issues critical to your department. You're furiously taking notes, but you can't keep up with the volume of information. What do you do?

   a. You think this is useless and a waste of your time. How does anyone in the company expect you to get this stuff when the speaker's talking like that?

   b. You listen and write as fast as you can. There's no way you can keep up, so you look around and find a co-worker whose notes you can borrow when the pitiful presentation is over. You daydream about the mountain village you visited last spring and start making plans to return.

   c. You listen for the main points and jot down key words. When you hear important information, you interrupt and say, "I didn't get that last point. Would you repeat that information?"

3. You've gathered several people together into the conference room for a scheduled training session. The consultant makes her opening remarks just as the window washers squeegee their way up to your floor. What do you do?

   a. Watch the window washers. How many times does a man climb twenty stories to clean a woman's windows? Could be actors on a movie set for all you know. Your big break is just a pane away.

   b. Take notes, listen to the squeegee, but alternate your concentration with the consultant. After all, she is $125 an hour and it's coming out of your department's budget.

   c. Say, "If you'll give me a moment, I can clear this up." Call Maintenance. If they can't move the window washers, then relocate to another room.

4. You played too hard last night. Today your stomach is a bit queasy, your back hurts and you want to go home. The company's best vendor will be here any minute. You're not sure if you can use her services, but you agreed to see her. Your secre-

tary pokes her head in and announces the vendor to you. What do you do?

a. Invite the woman to come in. She begins her presentation. You hear what she's saying, but you are so preoccupied with your queasiness, you can't listen to anything she says.

b. Invite her in. You aren't sure you can use her services or if you have the budget. She's here, so you might as well let her go through the motions. You look at your watch, and wonder when she'll finish.

c. You acknowledge that you are not at your best and your ability to listen is impaired. You invite her in. Say, "I'd like to listen to your presentation, and now is not a good time. Could we take a look at our calendars and reschedule this meeting?" You are also up front with her and let her know you need to take a close look at how her services fit your needs at this time.

5. David, your boss, is furious. He flies into your office and plunks a box full of green pens on your desk. "You never get the order straight. Every time I let you requisition office supplies, you mess things up." What do you do?

a. Open the box. Examine the pens while he's yelling. Sure enough, they're all green. You check every box. Suppose Red Cross could use green pens?

b. Say, "Yeah, well, a little color in here may be nice. At least they're not bright red. Reminds me of Irene Behrends, my eighth grade English teacher."

c. Say, "Let me repeat what you said. Every time I requisition office supplies, I mess things up."

6. Two months ago, you assigned a task force to study your company's long-distance telephone calls. You need to decide whether it would be to the company's advantage to get several 800 numbers. You expect them to come back with an affirmative answer. During their report, one member says, "Our company will be ready for an 800 number in six to eight months." What do you do?

    a. Go through your files. Try to figure out where they went wrong. Look at the ceiling. How could they be so misguided? Ask yourself why you hired them.

    b. Say, "Then, let's line it up right now. Beth, call the phone company. Tell them to hook us up."

    c. Say, "Six to eight months? That wasn't the answer I was expecting to hear. Tell me about your study and how you came to your conclusions."

7. You're an elementary school teacher. Your students finished a unit on space flight and one of them invites his uncle, a pilot, to come into the class and talk about piloting adventures. The uncle comes just before recess and he speaks in pilot jargon. What do you do?

    a. Say, "Thank you for coming. We're about ready for recess. You know kids. Can't keep them from having a little fun."

    b. Tell the kids to be polite and listen. Close the door. Pace up and down the aisles. Tap anyone who looks out the window. Sit at your desk. Cross out your guest speaker for next week and rewrite your lesson plans.

    c. Say, "I'm not sure we all know about 'vertical speed indicators.' Would you explain that?" Ask leading questions that you know will interest your students. Tell the students they'll get an extra ten minutes of recess after the adventure stories.

8. For years you worked in the machine shop. When you asked for a relocation into the offices, you were promoted to assistant manager. You work with Chuck, a wonderful, nice-looking young man. Sometimes he mumbles and he's hard to understand, but then that adorable blonde in word processing seems to hear him very well. Is it him, or do you have a hearing loss? What should you do?

    a. Ignore him. Sooner or later he'll learn how to speak plainly if he wants to stay in management. It's not your problem. Don't jeopardize your future by pointing out a weakness in a man.

   b. Say, "What is it about you, Chuck? You talk like a teenager, all vowels, no consonants. How am I supposed to understand you?"

   c. You get into a habit of paraphrasing what Chuck says, ensuring you've understood him, and you also say, "Chuck, when I listen to you, I think I might be missing something important. You could help me if you'd slow down some and speak a little louder."

9. You're working with top people in the company putting together a total quality management conference. When the conference is nearly planned, your boss wants you to add Dennis to your committee. In your opinion, Dennis throws negative energy into the group. During a meeting when the team is scheduling events and lining up speakers, Dennis asks, "Who's running the numbers on this? Has anyone thought to clear them through me?" What do you do?

   a. Stand up and walk away from Dennis. Pour yourself a cup of coffee. You are totally convinced he has nothing important to add to this group. Tune him out.

   b. Say, "Way to concentrate, Dennis. The numbers are in Ted's office, already approved. If you don't mind. . . ."

   c. Recognize that Dennis is probably an obsessive F on the SELF profile, and that might be why your boss wants him on the team. Say, "I have a copy of the budget right here. Ted's approved the numbers. It would be helpful if you'd take a close look at it to see if there's something we've overlooked."

10. You are sorting the laundry when your 15-year-old comes in and says, "Social Studies is a total waste of my time. I hate the teacher. We haven't talked about one relevant thing yet. Six weeks I've been in this class and I'm sick of it. I want to drop it from my schedule." What do you do?

   a. You continue sorting socks and think to yourself, "This kid has a crisis a day." You ignore what she's saying. Tell her to run upstairs and bring down the laundry. You have no time to waste today.

b. Say, "What do you mean, 'drop out'? Do you know how important that class is to your education? You can't expect everything in life to be fun and to your liking. Just buckle down and study. You can do it."

c. You are concerned about your daughter's problem. You want to get to the bottom of this issue and you realize she'll need to do that at her own pace and time. You try to understand her. Right now, it's more important to listen with your eyes and heart than with your ears. You give her the space she needs by simply repeating for understanding. You say, "You're telling me Social Studies is a real pain and a waste of time."

GRAND TOTALS

- Hearing is passive. You can hear and choose not to listen.

- Listening is active and takes energy. Your heart speeds up. Your blood circulates faster. Your temperature goes up.

- The listener can prevent the breakdown of communication. If you are speaking or listening, assume 51% responsibility for communication.

- Filters from the past influence your listening today. Be aware of your filters and create for yourself new attitudes that support good listening.

- Effective listeners recognize internal and external barriers, manage the barriers and listen with a purpose.

- Your eyes are your greatest instrument for listening. Listen beyond the words. The speaker's eyes, face, posture, and gestures are all talking to you.

- There are forces that drive you to listen the way you do. Are you an S, E, L, or F in most of your listening?

- Empathy is the deepest level of listening. You listen first to reflect your understanding of the other person. You listen with your ears, eyes and heart.

CAPTURING WHAT YOU'VE LEARNED

Things I've learned

_____

_____

Concepts I want to try

_____

_____

Great ideas I want to share with others

_____

_____

Things I want to know more about

_____

_____

Chapter Eight

◇

PROVEN WAYS TO MAKE DECISIONS AND SOLVE PROBLEMS

ELIMINATE NEGATIVE FEMALE STEREOTYPES

The days of the ditzy female are gone and the sooner the world notices the better. Shake yourself out of the old Dumb Dora model and into your sleek new power woman outfit. You can think with the best of them. You're smart, strong and ready to dive in and make decisions.

But before you do, erase the caricature of the dizzy dame who thinks with her heart, who shudders when you mention math or logic, who says one thing today and changes her mind—"Whoops, I'm sorry"—tomorrow. Draw in a cool keen woman who uses her feminine assets to enhance her problem-solving skills.

Test Yourself: Are You Feeding the Stereotypes Monster?

It's time to stave off stereotypes and let womankind's natural ability to problem-solve and make decisions shine. Do you have the confidence it takes to be an effective decision maker? Do you have the self-esteem to solve your company's problems? Take this quiz and find out.

1. There's a problem in your department with unauthorized breaks. The majority of your people are loitering in the break room. Three of your best workers are going through a divorce. You know how devastating that feels. They are taking longer breaks and spending more time on the phone with personal calls. Your supervisor calls you in to discuss strategy.

   "I want anyone abusing break privileges to get a warning," he says. You squeeze your hands together and begin:

   a. "You don't know how it feels to be getting a divorce, battling with lawyers and exes all day. Those women need their co-workers' support. I can't stand giving those poor women a warning."

   b. "Well, I tried clamping down last week, but then I changed my mind. I thought it would disrupt the continuity of the work group. Now that you mention it, maybe it would be a good idea to try some sort of restrictions again."

   c. Think for a moment and then say, "I agree that we need to do something to keep our break times in line. I'd like to consider what is best for the group as a whole. Maybe we can set up some Lunch and Learn sessions and bring in some speakers to talk about coping with lifestyle changes."

2. You're in the middle of a brainstorming session about an important new client, when your boss's secretary interrupts.

   "I'm afraid I made a mistake," she says. "I just realized I express-mailed that client portfolio to the wrong address."

   This portfolio is your boss's key strategy to keeping this new client happy.

   "Well," he says, throwing up his hands and looking at you and your co-workers, "we're sunk now. Does anybody have any ideas?"

You feel sorry for the secretary and nervous about your boss's volatile temper. You look around the table at your co-workers. You respond by:

a. Saying, "Anyone can make a mistake. I'm sure the client will understand and won't mind waiting an extra day."

b. Doodling on your tablet, waiting for someone else to come up with an idea.

c. Saying, "What about faxing a copy of the portfolio to a high-quality copy place and letting them copy it on good paper and deliver it?"

3. You have a million and one things to do and now one of your employees, Sonja, tells you there's a big problem down in the warehouse.

"What's wrong?" you ask.

"Everyone's unhappy," Sonja says.

You have a meeting scheduled in twenty minutes and you haven't eaten lunch yet and your phone's ringing and you say:

a. "I just can't stand it when everyone gets upset."

b. "This sounds like a big problem. I better get Ray in on it. He makes better decisions than I do."

c. "This sounds like a serious problem. I want to go to the warehouse and check it out and I need to wait until after the budget meeting."

4. You're in the break room and RaeAnn tells you about some problems going on in another section. She asks you to get involved in talking to some of the employees individually to see why they're so unhappy. You say:

a. "That happened in our department last year and half the people quit."

b. "I haven't had special training in this area, but I'd love to listen."

c. "I don't want to interfere in your department. However, if your supervisor wants to brainstorm with me, I'd love to help her."

5. Two years ago, you decided on a ten-hour work day. Now your employees are asking for flex-time. You haven't had a chance to analyze the situation. Your employees are eager for your reply. You tell them:

   a. "If everyone wants flex-time, I guess it's OK with me."

   b. "It took me a long time to come to that decision. I analyzed everything. I'm not giving it up."

   c. "Flex-time sounds worth looking into. But we need more information and a cost/benefit analysis." You delegate a team of people to prepare a report informing you about flex-time, and begin doing your own studies.

SCORING

If you picked all As, you are too deferring. You need support in proclaiming your own power. If you are a B person, you still have a case of the "less-than's." If you marked Cs, you have the confidence to make your own decisions. Use this chapter to hone your decision-making abilities.

ACCENTUATE POSITIVE FEMALE ADVANTAGES

Use your natural female advantages to add to your decision-making capabilities.

Here are some of your natural strengths:

CURIOSITY. Use your healthy curiosity as an information-gathering tool. Listen to your inner voice and your intuition, and let them play a guiding role in your decision making.

CREATIVITY. Your creative spirit leads you to new paths, new ways to making decisions. Let it flow. Don't be afraid to show people how wonderfully creative you really are.

FOCUS. Stay focused on all aspects of problem solving and decision making. Your ability to stick with a problem and see it to completion gives you a strong advantage.

PREVENTION. Your alertness and listening abilities will keep problems from recurring.

HOW DECISION MAKING AND PROBLEM SOLVING WORK: THE STEPS TO EXCELLENCE

Cassie feels something is wrong with her department but she doesn't know what. People are grumbling more, coming in late and not getting work done on time. Plus, there seems to be quite a turnover in secretarial support staff. She talks to her best friend Sheila in the Art Department. Sheila says, "You must be imagining things. Our group is really getting along well. You're probably just having a bad day."

But Ellen, a secretary in Cassie's department, tells Cassie while they are in the restroom that "everybody feels so unhappy."

Cassie doesn't know what to think. As the department manager, she needs to be in tune with her employees. Yet she doesn't want to overreact.

DEFINING THE ROOT OF THE PROBLEM IS KEY TO THE DECISION-MAKING PROCESS.

Fast Fact
Decision making is a complex process, starting with information gathering, analysis, and weighing the alternatives.

Action
Approximately 20% of decision making goes through a well-thought-out complex process. Cassie needs to get comfortable with the nine steps in the decision-making process.

The Nine-Step Path to Excellent Decision Making

STEP 1: BECOME AWARE OF THE PROBLEM. Tune in to the mood and attitude of those around you. Pay attention to the grapevine. Sometimes the information you receive might not seem significant. Don't discount its importance.

Maintain a pipeline of communication and seek out internal and external communications. Be watchful for problem signals.

Problem Signals:

- ♦ Persistent lateness.
- ♦ Taking long breaks.
- ♦ Lack of motivation.
- ♦ Absenteeism.
- ♦ Sloppy work.
- ♦ Minor accidents.

STEP 2: GET TO THE ROOT OF THE PROBLEM. Cassie decides to ask around to try to understand the office moodiness.

"Why is everyone so down?" Cassie asks Norma, one of the secretaries.

"We hate the new rule that you can't have anything on your desk," Norma says. "How can we get our work done without a cup of coffee, extra paper, and so forth? I like to eat and look at my son's picture. This new system is just terrible."

Often a problem will have a physical symptom. It's easier to say, "I hate having to keep my desk a certain way," than to admit, "I feel like nobody cares about me."

Are you solving the symptom of the problem or the root? It's easy to fix the cosmetics and the surface woes, but harder to dig deep and find out what's really bothering people.

How do you sift through the symptoms and find the whole story? If you sense a problem brewing, pay close attention. Watch for physical symptoms. Ask questions about how the disgruntled group is feeling. What is wrong? What would they want to fix? Pay close attention to their answers. Take notes and think about the information. Then ask more questions. What else is wrong? Is there something else I need to know? What else is really getting on their nerves?

Most initial complaints are a test to see if you can handle the situation without being judgmental or negative.

Cassie needs to ask more questions of Norma and the other secretaries.

"What if we figured out how to allow some personal items on your desks? Would that help?" Cassie asks.

"It's not just the desks—it's the managers. They act like they don't have the time of day for us. Ever since the merger, they rush past us and dump work on our desks like we're machines."

Cassie needs to hear what Norma is really saying. "Since the merger, everything seems different. We no longer have the camaraderie we did, where the bosses knew everyone and walked through each morning, greeting us all, asking how things were going. It's a little thing, but it means a lot. Now I feel like we're part of the furniture. Nobody cares. Nobody asks how we're doing. People just pile up the work and hold out their hand so they'll get it back fast."

STEP 3: GATHER INFORMATION. Now that Cassie knows the real problem—the support staff feel undervalued and need more attention—what can she do about it?

She can talk to as many as possible.

When you are solving problems for a group, get their input. Ask them how they would solve the problem. Ask for many ideas. Write down each idea without judgment. You are simply compiling a resource file that you will use later.

Cassie can interview the new managers and find out about their managerial style. Are they willing to spend more time talking to the support staff, to give them the recognition, appreciation and respect they deserve? And what is the best way to go about this? What about the individuals who have a personal assistant? How do they treat their assistants? Do they praise them and help them advance?

Once you have found the problem, you need to gather information that will help you to solve it.

This is a good time to reach out to other people. Focus on people who are affected by the potential decision. Make sure you know all sides of the issue.

People play a key role in your becoming a power problem solver. Be "people plentiful" when you gather information. Talk to people:

♦ Whom the decision affects.

♦ Who help implement the decision.

♦ Who have gone through similar problems, within your company.

◆ Who have struggled through similar problems, from other companies.

STEP 4. CONSIDER POSSIBLE SOLUTIONS. Now that you've gathered the information, it's time to use "what if" thinking to generate a ton of solutions.

◆ What if you showed a funny movie each lunch hour?

◆ What if you offered flex-time so people wouldn't have to worry about getting there at 7 a.m. every morning?

◆ What if you dismissed people who were chronically late?

◆ What if you made exceptions for people who are going through divorces and other trauma?

◆ What if you trained managers to give their employees positive and consistent feedback?

◆ What if the company scheduled time for managers to have daily contact with their support staff?

◆ What if you trained the support staff to support each other, to build work and energy together?

These are a few of the "what if" solutions you can generate in this intense creative period.

Once you've brainstormed, now get logical. Do a costs-rewards analysis for each decision and see what looks the best to you.

For example, let's say you wanted to analyze:

Training support staff to support each other.

Costs might include: Training money, training time, management might feel threatened, staff still might feel that it's not enough, and might need even more management support.

Rewards might include: A more autonomous and empowered group of workers, a higher sense of self-esteem leading to increased productivity.

If your decision affects other people, do this costs-rewards analysis as a group. You need at least one other person involved to keep you focused.

Think beyond the obvious financial costs and rewards. Look

closely at the costs. Are you willing to pay the costs? Are the rewards greater than the costs?

Ask yourself:

- What does it cost me if I do it?
- What does it cost me if I don't do it?

Keep your analysis paper handy so you can stay focused and remember the rewards you expect to achieve.

STEP 5. SELECT THE BEST COURSE OF ACTION. Cassie feels like she's been swimming in the support pool! She's thought about the problem from many angles. She's analyzed each potential solution, pro and con. She's gotten advice from a number of people involved. Her boss has given her some limitations which include:

- Don't spend more than $1000.
- Don't take much of the manager's time on a weekly basis.
- Do something that shows short-term results.

Like Cassie, most of us have to make decisions with some less-than-ideal limitations. One key to decision making is realizing the strengths of each alternative and going for the strongest choice.

When making a decision, ask yourself:

- What new skills will we need?
- How will we acquire those skills? (seminars, books, tapes)
- What new equipment will we need?
- Do we have the right financial resources?

Then answer these questions:

- Why does something need to be done?
- Who will do it and when?
- Where will it take place?

◆ How will it be done? (individually, groups, workshops, training manuals, and so forth)

◆ Is this compatible with other systems and policies?

◆ Do we have enough people and equipment to make this work?

◆ How will people respond?

◆ Whom will it make mad and how mad?

Each of these questions help you get clearer focus and greater understanding of the potential impact of your decision.

Cassie decides to train the managers to give employees weekly feedback. She contacts an outside speaker who does wonderful motivational workshops. This speaker will train the managers on giving positive feedback. Cassie designs a simple form, one that the managers agree they can easily fill out and one that the support staff okayed as meeting their needs. She prints copies of this form and reviews the feedback system with the bosses, then later with the support staff.

STEP 6: MAKE YOUR DECISION WORK. Cassie's made her decision and now she's plagued with a batch of negative "what ifs." She drives home from work and imagines all the support staff quitting because they didn't get the feedback they needed. And the managers are so irritated, they ask for Cassie's resignation.

Your mind may be crawling with doubts after you make your decision. Remember these three energizers:

◆ Don't succumb to negative thinking.

◆ Have faith in yourself. You've researched and thought out the decision. Now put your energy into making it work.

◆ Keep your focus on the rewards.

STEP 7: DIRECT THE IMPLEMENTATION. Cassie is nervous. The managers have gathered and she's ready to tell them about her decision, as well as ask for help with implementation. She clears her throat and makes a light-hearted comment.

"Many of you have been involved in solving the problem of our support staff's low morale and high turnover. You know we've been trying to come up with a solution that is easy to implement and doesn't take too much of your time. I'm happy to say, we've found it."

Cassie then tells them about the seminar and goes over the implementation details.

Because Cassie told the managers the reasoning first, they easily listened to and accepted the remedy.

Implementation Tools

- When implementing your decision, tell people the reason first and the remedy second. This avoids selective listening that blocks understanding.

- Set up a test situation.

    Cassie might tell the staff, "We'll try this new system for six weeks."

    Limiting the initial time period reduces the threat of change.

- Set up an implementation schedule.

    Know the who, what, where, why and how of implementation. You worked through these in the planning stages.

- Monitor the results of the test decision. Use individual and group feedback.

- Adjust and improve the decision.

    Use as many avenues of communication as possible when implementing your decision. Individual conversations, meetings, memos, letters, posters, and newsletters all help make people a part of the decision.

STEP 8: EVALUATE THE RESULTS. Three months have passed since Cassie's motivational training course. The managers are supposed to consistently look for opportunities to show appreciation as well as make at least five or ten minutes a day available for personal contact.

In evaluating the success of the decision, Cassie needs to remind herself of the desired results: Has morale improved? Has turnover decreased? Is productivity stable?

She needs to find out if the managers are actually keeping to their promised weekly time schedules and filling out the contact sheets.

♦ Have any new problems come up that she didn't think of before implementation?

♦ If she needs to modify the plan, how will this affect other aspects?

♦ What worked? What didn't?

Cassie can quickly review her cost-rewards analysis. Are the rewards still overweighing the costs?

Walking around and talking to people is a great way to get feedback on your decisions. Create an interesting evaluation form and ask people to fill it out. For those who filled out the evaluation, let them know the results of their input.

STEP 9: USE WHAT YOU'VE LEARNED TO GUIDE FUTURE DECISION MAKING. Cassie learned that half the managers did what they agreed on. She learned that the support staff generally feel better, but they would work more effectively if they had a greater sense of commitment and collaboration among themselves.

Cassie believes that empowering the support staff through some self-esteem and motivational courses might have been more successful in the long term.

Here are some questions to use when you analyze the results of what you've learned:

♦ If I had to do this over, what would I do differently?

♦ Would I have taken longer to gather the information?

♦ Would I have communicated differently?

♦ What would make the implementation easier and more effective?

♦ What worked well?

♦ What could have been better?

Using all this information, Cassie is better prepared to tackle her next long-term decision.

SETTING PRIORITIES, SOLVING PROBLEMS AND DELEGATING THE TASK

Lora just returned from a business trip and her desk is piled with mail, her phone is ringing off the hook, and she has a list of people wanting to talk to her. Help! She feels overwhelmed. She doesn't have time to handle every item that needs her attention. In fact, she doesn't even have time to think through every item that is pulling on her. She plunges in by answering the phone. One of her supervisors is having problems in her department. Lora leaves her office to visit this supervisor before looking through the stack of messages on her desk. Later, when she returns to her office, she sees an angry note from her manager, asking her why she missed the important personnel meeting this morning. Lora sits in her chair, feeling sick. She thinks she made the wrong decision, visiting with that supervisor. She wishes she had gone through her list, prioritized her workload and delegated some of her tasks to others.

UNDERSTANDING THE DIFFERENCE BETWEEN THE URGENT AND THE IMPORTANT IS THE KEY TO KEEPING YOUR FOCUS. EIGHTY PERCENT OF THE DECISIONS YOU MAKE ARE SPUR OF THE MOMENT.

Fast Fact

Prioritizing and weeding out are crucial skills. Think "delegate" before you get lost in doing everything.

Action

Lora needs to ask herself:

What is urgent and what is important?

What needs to be done?

When does it need to be done?

Does it need to be done at all?

Second, she needs to ask:

What must *I* do?

What needs to be done that others can do for me? (I need their help.)

What are others' responsibilities that I can help them with?

What *must* be done by others?

Often women think "DO" before they think "DELEGATE." Train yourself to know the difference between the task and the goal.

Do Versus Delegate

When should you plunge in and DO something? When should you take charge and DELEGATE? When should you choose to defer or not do at all? Often it's a tricky decision. Here are some tips to keep you focused:

+ Know your boundaries. What is your primary task? What is your secondary task? Stay focused and in your area.

+ Take the time to train people to do completed staff work. Delegate by degrees. For example, your task is to do a report.

Assess the skills of the person you are delegating to and use these options:

Phase I   Ask her to gather the information for you, then you write the report.

Phase II   Have her gather the information and write the report. Then you revise the report and sign it.

Phase III   Have her gather the information, write the report and sign it. You initial the completed document.

Phase IV   Have her gather the information, write the report, sign it and send it out. Ask her to send you a copy of the completed report.

Have a sense of the "big picture." Plan for the long term. This helps you stay goal-directed vs. task-directed. Another part of the "big picture" is preparing someone to take your place. Women are frequently by passed for promotions because they are seen as indispensable in their current positions. "No one else can do Carly's job," is the company perception that stands in the way of your advancement.

Test Yourself: Are You a Doer or a Delegator?

Here is a vital "to do" list. What must you do? What can you delegate? What can you defer and what doesn't need to be done?

In the space provided, put a **"D"** by any tasks you can delegate. Write **"DO"** by the tasks you feel you must perform yourself. Write **DE** by the tasks you can defer and **X** by those tasks you won't do at all.

_____ a. Your phone is ringing.

_____ b. You have a huge headache and you're starved. You're not sure if you can operate much longer without some nourishment. It will take you at least 20 minutes to go out and get some healthy food.

_____ c. The copy machine is broken and your secretary wants to know if you want to repair it yourself or call the repairman. Your boss has drastically reduced your office supply budget, and you can often fix the machine. But it takes at least 20 minutes to fix it, and another ten minutes to get cleaned up and presentable afterwards.

_____ d. On your desk, you have the following messages:

_____ One from your best friend.

_____ One from Jim, an important client, marked priority.

_____ One from a vendor who says he's got a four-hour sale going on.

_____ e. Your assistant rushes in to tell you that Ann needs your authorization immediately for a trip to Dayton. Airline tickets are going up tonight and she's got a fare that will save the company $500. You don't know the details of the trip and to find out will take at least ten minutes.

_____ f. Your boss sends a message that he wants you to attend an important marketing meeting tomorrow. To do things right, you need to proofread the latest marketing report and make sure it's accurate before the meeting. This will take at least 30 minutes.

_____ g. The head of print production leaves a message that his key assistant is unhappy and looking for a job outside your company. He wants you to come down and see if you can persuade the guy to stay. Wow, this guy is hard to talk to and it will take at least 25 minutes.

Shine up your decision making and prioritizing skills with these *delegate, do, defer* or *forget it* answers.

a. **D**elegate. Unless you are the only person in the office, others can answer the phone, screen your calls, take messages. If you are alone, let electronic equipment take care of your phone interruptions.

b. **DO.** Take care of yourself. Get some nourishment before you tackle your other problems.

c. **D**elegate. Your job as a manager does not include being a repair person. The price of hiring repair help may be less than the cost of you doing it yourself. While you spend time repairing that machine, you are neglecting other important tasks.

d. Manage your time wisely as you choose your response to these three messages:

   DEfer   Call you best friend later.

   DO   You need to work with the client. Your clients always have high priority.

   X   Ignore this "urgent" sale. Sales come and go. If these prices can't wait four hours, they're probably not worth it.

e. **D**elegate. Ask your assistant to call Ann for the details and to submit these for your approval. Remember, it is not your responsibility to get the details.

f. **D**elegate or **DE**fer. Do this in the evening or first thing in the morning. Or have your assistant do the proofreading.

g. **D**elegate. This is the print production's key assistant, not yours. He needs to work on the problem. You are willing to mentor him, but delegate the task to him.

TAKE CONTROL: HOW TO BOOST YOUR VALUE TO THE COMPANY

Evelyn wants to be a manager but becomes paralyzed when it comes to decision making. She just can't stand to make a mistake.

"What if everyone blames me?" she worries. Because of her inaction, she hasn't received a promotion in years.

PART OF MAKING DECISIONS IS TAKING RISKS. THE MORE DECISIONS YOU MAKE, THE GREATER THE POSSIBILITY FOR MAKING MISTAKES.

Fast Fact
Learn to stay out of the pitfalls of decision making and you'll boost your visibility and value to your company.

Action
Evelyn needs to go through the decision-making process and learn how to make decisions that work.

Seven Secrets of Picture-Perfect Decisions

1. **READY, AIM, FOCUS.** Don't underestimate the importance of your decision. Look at the big picture and make sure you have clear sight of everything your decision affects. Think of the short-term and long-term results of your decision and anticipate problems and side effects.

2. **WIDE ANGLE LENS.** Don't narrow your focus just to meet your needs or please those on your team. Think of all the options. Imagine a wide range of options and figure out how each affects the picture.

3. **COMING OUT OF THE DARKROOM.** Take time to see the light that others shed. Input from other people helps you create a better

decision. You don't have to do everything or know everything. Tap into the valuable resources of those around you.

4. ACTION SHOTS. Make your decision while things are vibrant and in motion. Don't stop everything so you can spend hours analyzing and researching the minute aspects of the decision. Don't procrastinate, hoping things will somehow be perfect another day. Make the best of what you have now. Give your decision impact and vitality by making it in a timely manner.

5. SCENES FROM THE FUTURE. Just because something worked once, doesn't mean you should keep making the same decision. Each situation demands fresh consideration. Use brainstorming techniques to keep your creative flow. Ask advice from other people. Open yourself up to new ideas and odd-angled approaches.

6. SHOOTING FROM A DIFFERENT ANGLE. Often a decision that once inspired and activated hundreds of people outlives its effectiveness. Be a positive force by being alert to dead decisions. Once you make a decision, let go of ego attachment. Be clear in your overview. If the original decision is fading, what will work next? Be the one to come up with the clearest picture and the perfect angle.

7. MAKING SURE SOMETHING DEVELOPS. Not only do you need your decision-making focus, you also need follow-through and implementation abilities. Use your communication skills to let everyone know what the decision is and who will be carrying it out. Build a team of people involved in making your decision come to life. These tips give you the best shot at being a great decision maker.

Take Two: How Is Your Decision-Making Ability?

Now that you're comfortable making decisions, take this test again and see how you've changed your views.

1. There's a problem in your department with unauthorized breaks. The majority of your people are loitering in the break room. Three of your best workers are going through a divorce. You know how devastating that feels. They are taking longer

breaks and spending more time on the phone with personal calls. Your supervisor calls you in to discuss strategy.

"I want anyone abusing break privileges to get a warning," he says. You squeeze your hands together and begin:

a. "You don't know how it feels to be getting a divorce and battling with lawyers and exes all day. Those women need their co-workers' support. I can't stand giving those poor women a warning."

b. "Well, I tried clamping down last week, but then I changed my mind. I thought it would disrupt the continuity of the work group. Now that you mention it, maybe it would be a good idea to try some sort of restrictions again."

c. Think for a moment and then say, "I agree that we need to do something to keep our break times in line. I'd like to consider what is best for the group as a whole. Maybe we can set up some "Lunch and Learn" sessions and bring in some speakers to talk about coping with lifestyle changes."

2. You're in the middle of a brainstorming session about an important new client, when your boss's secretary interrupts.

"I'm afraid I made a mistake," she says. "I just realized I express-mailed that client portfolio to the wrong address."

That portfolio was your boss's key strategy to keeping this new client happy.

"Well," he says, throwing up his hands and looking at you and your co-workers, "we're sunk now. Does anybody have any ideas?"

You feel sorry for the secretary and nervous about your boss's volatile temper. You look around the table at your co-workers. You respond by:

a. Saying, "Anyone can make a mistake. I'm sure the client will understand and won't mind waiting an extra day."

b. Doodling on your tablet and waiting for someone else to come up with an idea.

c. Saying, "What about faxing a copy of the portfolio to a high-quality copy place and letting them copy it on good paper and deliver it?"

3. You have a million and one things to do and now one of your employees, Sonja, tells you there's a big problem down in the warehouse.

   "What's wrong?" you ask.

   "Everyone's unhappy," Sonja says.

   You have a meeting scheduled in twenty minutes and you haven't eaten lunch yet and your phone's ringing and you say:

   a. "I just can't stand it when everyone gets upset."

   b. "This sounds like a big problem. I better get Ray in on it. He makes better decisions than I do."

   c. "This sounds like a serious problem. I want to go to the warehouse and check it out and I need to wait until after the budget meeting."

4. You're in the break room and RaeAnn tells you about some problems going on in another section. She asks you to get involved in talking to some of the employees individually to see why they're so unhappy. You say:

   a. "That happened in our department last year and half the people quit."

   b. "I haven't had special training in this area, but I'd love to listen."

   c. "I don't want to interfere in your department. However, if your supervisor wants to brainstorm with me, I'd love to help her."

5. Two years ago, you decided on a ten-hour work day. Now your employees are asking for flex-time. You haven't had a chance to analyze the situation. Your employees are eager for your reply. You tell them:

   a. "If everyone wants flex-time, I guess it's OK with me."

   b. "It took me a long time to come to that decision. I analyzed everything. I'm not giving it up."

   c. "Flex-time sounds worth looking into. But we need more information and a cost/benefit analysis." You delegate a team of people to prepare a report informing you about flex-time, and begin doing your own studies.

Did you "C the light" and have the increased confidence you need to make powerful decisions? Adopting a strong decision-making style takes time, so be patient with yourself.

GRAND TOTALS

Now you can make your decisions with confidence and logic. You have the tools to make decisions that affect the future, and the ability to quickly prioritize tasks that require instant decisions. You have worked through the components of a good decision and you have learned the tricks to making decisions that work.

- ◆ You know that decision making requires fresh thinking and risk taking.
- ◆ You know how to judge other people's needs and how to speak to them in a persuasive and meaningful style.
- ◆ You can singlehandedly make a decision as you rely on the valuable input of others.
- ◆ You understand how to get to the root of a problem and how to analyze the possible solutions.
- ◆ You know the communication network it takes to research a problem and implement your decision.
- ◆ You know how to learn from past decisions.
- ◆ You know how to prioritize tasks and how to delegate.

CAPTURING WHAT YOU'VE LEARNED

Things I've learned

_____

_____

Concepts I want to try

_____

_____

Great ideas I want to share with others

_____

_____

Things I want to know more about

_____

_____

Chapter Nine

SUREFIRE WAYS TO FIRE UP YOUR PRESENTATION SKILLS

The quickest way for you to gain greater visibility and credibility is through stand-up presentations. As a speaker, YOU are the message. As a woman, you need to understand that everything about you speaks.

Sure, your words are important. Your volume and tone of voice contribute. But your listeners are also taking in vocabulary, gestures, posture, eye contact and movements.

Presentation skills are a key to your business success. But do you know the facts and fictions of the presentation process?

PRESENTATION FACT OR FALLACY: TEST YOURSELF

1. You don't need presentation skills if you're just talking to your co-workers or your boss. **True/False?**

2. You should never volunteer to speak. **True/False?**

3. As a speaker, you can't control your audience's attention span. **True/False?**

4. Using stories and anecdotes in your speech gets your audience off-track. **True/False?**

5. Humor makes your presentation seem frivolous. **True/False?**

6. Just standing in front of people makes them pay attention to everything you are saying. **True/False?**

7. The best speeches are crammed with facts and details. **True/False?**

8. You'll know when you've made it as a speaker: You'll be perfectly calm before each speech. **True/False?**

9. If you know your subject well enough, you shouldn't have to practice your speech more than once. **True/False?**

10. Gestures are nice but not necessary for your presentation. **True/False?**

If you answered "False" for everything, you have a basic understanding of the dynamics of presentations. Read on to find out how this understanding can work for you. If you answered "True," you'll be delighted by the information this chapter gives you to enhance your presentation skills.

WHO'S AFRAID? MAKING FEAR WORK FOR YOU

"I'd rather ride the elevator in my underwear than give a presentation."

"I'd rather do without chocolate for three weeks than speak in front of people."

"Cutting the lawn with my teeth would be less stressful than getting up to talk in front of a group."

Is fear keeping you from gaining the visibility you need? Is anxiety around speaking blocking your advancement and promotion?

Speak up for yourself and use your fear as an ally instead of a villain.

Delia has been asked to give a presentation to the department heads in her area of expertise, the new computer program. Delia is smart, articulate and knows this program fully.

"I can't speak, I'll make a fool of myself, nobody will listen, it'll ruin my career," she tells Mary at lunch.

FEAR OF PUBLIC SPEAKING RANKS IN THE TOP TEN OF WOMEN'S BUSINESS FEARS.

Fact
It's normal to have fears about speaking. You may share these fears:

+ Fear of being center stage
+ Fear of the unknown
+ Fear of risking damage to self-esteem
+ Fear of making mistakes in front of others

Action
Do not let these fears silence you. Build your presentation skills and you will diminish your fears. Preparation and practice are the keys to fear busting.

Three Tricks for Taming Fear

1. CONFRONT FEAR. Ask yourself, What am I afraid of? Listen to the voices in your head and notice what they are saying. Write down every fear you can think of. Then wad up the paper, take it home and burn it in your sink.

2. SEE SUCCESS. Create a mind-set of success. See yourself in vivid detail giving a wildly successful presentation. By doing lots of mental rehearsals, you program your success at a subconscious level.

3. BE YOUR OWN CHEERLEADER. As you get ready for your presentation, say to yourself, "I am the best person for this presentation. They are really going to love this."

WHO'S WHO AND WHAT'S WHAT: KNOW YOUR AUDIENCE

Marie's supervisor asked her to talk to a luncheon meeting of business people to promote her company's Public Relations capabilities.

Marie agreed and put together some generic public relations information and felt ready to talk. But when she got to the restaurant, she saw a sign that said, "Welcome Public Relations Society."

Marie felt the sweat decorate her forehead. Her feet wanted to run back to the car. She hadn't prepared for such a sophisticated audience!

KNOWING YOUR AUDIENCE IS CRUCIAL TO YOUR SUCCESSFUL PRESENTATION.

Fast Fact

When you receive an invitation to speak, the first things you want to know are about the audience. Without understanding their concerns and needs, you cannot communicate effectively with them.

Action

Create an Audience Analysis sheet. Fill it out and study it each time you need to make a presentation.

Analyze Your Listeners: Questions to Ask

- What is the profession of your audience?
- Why are they coming? Did they sign up voluntarily? Are they drafted? Are they missing valuable business time or coming on days off?
- What values do they hold?
- What is the gender mix? What percentage are men/women?
- What is the average age? Use stories and anecdotes that will mesh with their experience.
- What do they expect you to say? Read the preprogram publicity and deliver everything promised.

- After your presentation, what should the audience do, think, feel or believe?

- What size group are you addressing? This will affect your tone. Ten or fewer people comprise an intimate group. A small group is 11–25, an average group is 26–50. More than 50 listeners comprises a large audience. You will vary your presentation style according to each size audience.

- What is the purpose of the event? What is the meeting planner expecting from you?

- Is the audience informed or uninformed? How much knowledge does it have on your topic? Are there terms or jargon the audience don't know?

- What time of day are you addressing the audience? You'll need livelier activities during the after-lunch period or the cocktail hour.

Answer every question and create a focus sentence that encapsulates your audience.

"My audience is comprised of CPAs who are required to attend a human relations workshop."

"My audience is comprised of businesswomen wanting to know how human relations issues affect their companies."

Keep your audience description in front of you and gear your speech to meet your audience's needs.

PRESENTATION PREPARATION: HOW TO GET RAVE REVIEWS

Sure, Kay Keller, an international speaker with National Seminars Group, gets a little nervous before presentations. But her nervousness heightens her speaking ability and gives her energy. How does she manage her nervousness and not let it paralyze her?

"I plan every inch of my presentation," Keller says. "Prior proper planning prohibits the possibility of a pitifully poor presentation."

How to Use Grand Openings to Connect with Your Audience

Karen has practiced for her presentation all week. She analyzed her audience and planned, prepared and practiced. She flooded herself with positive self-talk. "I am the best person to give this speech," she proclaims to herself.

She walks into the conference room designated for her presentation. Her co-workers are clustered around the big table, talking comfortably.

Karen clears her throat and waits for a moment.

"I'm here to tell you about the new policies we're implementing during the merger period," she begins. She notices the room isn't that quiet. Her audience isn't focused on her.

"These policies are important to all of us . . . ," she goes on, wondering how she can get everyone's attention.

JUST BECAUSE YOU'RE READY TO SPEAK, DOESN'T MEAN YOUR AUDIENCE IS READY TO LISTEN.

Fast Fact
Get the audience members' attention so they will want to listen.

Action
Open with something interesting, personal or provocative. After you get your audience's attention, get their support and interest. Initiate a sincere relationship with your audience.

Ask yourself:
- What will catch your listeners' attention?
- What will hold their interest?
- What action do you want and how will you get it?

Make your opening work for you. Use an anecdote, a story, a participatory exercise, a provocative sentence, or a fascinating statistic.

Your opening establishes:
- Rapport with the audience.
- Style and tone.

+ Subject matter.
+ Your credibility.

IN THE BEGINNING: SEVEN DOs AND DON'Ts FOR ESTABLISHING AUDIENCE RAPPORT. The opening is the most important part of your speech. Use these tips for immediate audience approval.

1. DO begin with energy and stay upbeat all the way through.

2. DON'T ever begin your presentation with an apology. This sets a negative tone and distances the audience. Phrases such as these are sure ways to put you in a bad light:

   + I'm sorry this speech isn't as polished as I'd like, but my plane was late last night and I . . .

   + I really have to apologize for the quality of the overheads but my regular print shop was closed last night when I finally got around to this.

3. DON'T hand out printed information at the beginning of your talk. This destroys the mood and distracts the audience. Hand out written data either as you come to it or at the end of the presentation.

4. DON'T begin by thanking everyone and their cocker spaniel. Who cares? "I'd like to thank Joe for inviting me and my department head for giving me this day off and my mother for teaching me to speak. . . ."

5. DO use humor. "Have you heard the one about the traveling salesman? . . ." Watch out for jokes. Most are worn and torn and people have heard them. Humor is wonderful; jokes are marginal.

6. Get your audience involved with you, with each other and the subject matter immediately. If you're giving a talk on stress, invite people to "Stand and introduce yourself to three other people. Tell them what is stressing you." This enlivens the room, builds energy and gets the audience personally involved and excited about the topic. Here are two activities that will energize and involve your audience:

Buzz Groups

- Form groups of three to four people.

- Clearly state the problem or issue (preferably related to your presentation) you want the groups to discuss. For example, "Your company has a new mandate that 50% of its employees will be in carpools by next June. There is great employee resistance to this idea. How can you help solve this problem?"

- Ask each person to raise her hand, pointing the index finger to the ceiling. "At the count of three, point to the person in your group you want to begin the discussion." The person who receives the most "fingers" begins the discussion.

- Circulate among the groups, making sure they are on track.

- Let them know when there are two minutes left.

- Call time.

- Request a brief report from each group. Ask each speaker to add only those ideas that haven't yet been covered.

- Process the information, summarize and draw it into your presentation.

Problem/Solution

- Have each person write down a problem they are experiencing, related to the topic of your presentation. For example, "What problems do you have with time management?"

- Have each person find a partner.

- Establish a mentor/protégée relationship. The protégée shares her problem with the mentor. The mentor has two minutes to come up with as many solutions as possible. The protégée writes everything down without comment.

- Switch roles and go through the process again.

- Call time and get some responses from the group to tie in with your presentation.

7. For this moment in time, you are the STAR, not the housekeeper. Don't talk about mundane housekeeping issues in the

opening. Let the meeting planner do that, or do it before the first break.

How to Give Your Presentation a Great Body

Sandra has just wowed her audience at the Business Communicators luncheon with a wonderful story about a man who talked only with gestures. The room relaxed—even the guys with the beepers, portable phones, three-piece suits and four Gold cards were following along—raising their hands at the right moment and laughing at the end.

"This is just one way to communicate," Sandra says, when the story ends. "What I'll talk about today are the different ways our clients communicate with us. But first, I need to tell you something funny that happened yesterday at work."

Sandra launches into another story. She is a wonderful storyteller, but she notices halfway through that two people at the front table glance at their watches.

WITHOUT AN ORGANIZED CLEAR BODY, YOUR SPEECH LOSES ITS APPEAL.

Fast Fact

The body of your speech reveals its content and your intent. The more clear and logical you are, the better the audience understands your points.

Action

Sandra needs to make sure her stories add to the content rather than obscure it.

Sometimes organizing a speech is daunting. Don't be tied and chained by a numbered outline. Have fun creating clusters of associated words. If you're talking about preventive health, write "health" in the center of the page (colored paper adds a nice touch). Then give yourself five or ten minutes and write down all the words you can think of. Let yourself go on tangents. Circle each word, draw lines to connect the words, or squares. Make the page visual and appealing. From this circus of ideas, write each separate idea on index cards. Now put them in order and begin your body.

To give your speech a really great body, you need to:

- *Establish the main topics.* People learn by repetition. Tell your audience the main topics you are discussing at the beginning of the body and again in the conclusion.

- *Order your topics.* Put these topics in a logical order and use transitions to help move the audience from one to the next.

  For example, if you have three main topics, you might say, "First, we'll discuss communicating with clients. . . ." "Second, we'll talk about communicating with co-workers. . . ." "Finally, let's discuss the issues involved in communicating with vendors."

  Using transition words, such as "first, second, then, finally, next," eases your audience from one thought to the next.

- *Support your topics.* Use facts, not opinions, to support your topics. Give concrete details, rather than vagaries. The more specific you are, the better your audience will understand your points. For example, "It's important to be a good communicator," is a vague sentence based on opinion. "When you are a good communicator, your clients know where you stand, and feel comfortable approaching you," is more concrete. It tells you specifically the reasons to communicate well.

How to Create Happy Endings Every Time

As she nears the end of her talk, Andie starts feeling nervous. People are fidgeting and she wants desperately to get out and get the talk over with.

"Well, I guess that's all," she says, as soon as she finishes the final topic. She walks out of the room as fast as she can.

USE YOUR ENDING TO LEAVE A STRONG POSITIVE IMPRESSION ON YOUR LISTENERS.

Fast Fact
The final impression makes an impact on the audience. Make sure you are selling yourself as well as recapping your speech.

Action
Don't give away your power by acting scared at the end of your speech. You are creating an impression of knowledge, strength and skill that must be good to the last drop. Every word you speak sells you and your topic.

Choose a powerful and memorable way to end your speech. Don't rush. Don't start feeling guilty that you've taken up time. Shine out with confidence as you come to a strong conclusion. Remember your goal: How do you want the audience to think, believe, or feel when your speech is over?

Here are some endings that reinforce learning and create a positive feeling:

+ Restate opinion or purpose.
+ Summarize.
+ Recommend.

Add a dynamic "call for action" to your conclusion, urging your listeners either to a specific course of action, to carry on the feeling of your speech, or to remember what they've learned.

CLEAR SPEAK: PRACTICE MAKES FOR PERFECT PRESENTATIONS

Fran is ready for the big moment. She strides up to the platform confident and in control. As she opens her speech, she notices her friend Mona gesturing to her—Mona is acting like a monkey with an itch. Fran wishes she'd settle down and stop trying to distract her.

On break, Mona rushes up.

"Fran, I was trying to tell you, you have a tag hanging from under your arm. And you're playing with your hair."

Fran reaches up and touches the price tag of her new suit. She wonders if her audience was smiling because of the dangling tag.

YOU HAVE THIRTY SECONDS TO CREATE A POSITIVE FIRST IMPRESSION.

Fast Fact

Your audience will form an impression before you start speaking. Approach your audience with enthusiasm. Walk confidently, shoulders back. Take ownership of your space. Your voice, posture, dress and style create the impression the listeners carry with them. Be present and strong every moment you are in the room.

Action

Go over every part of your speech in advance.

The Power of Practice

You are the commander of the room while you speak. Project that authority and control by practicing these elements of your presentation.

TAKE CONTROL THROUGH SPACE MANAGEMENT. *Take up plenty of space,* with your stance, your movement and your gestures. Don't act timid or shy. *Stand with your feet six to eight inches apart.* Practice feeling comfortable in this stance. Practice at home or in restaurants striding forcefully across the room.

MAKE YOUR SOUND SYSTEM WORK FOR YOU. How you say something is more important than what you say. Tape record yourself having a conversation with a friend, spouse, boss, peer, parent, employee. Listen to your voice tone. Which conversation projects the tone of voice that sounds best?

Listen for speech mannerisms such as fillers: uh, er, um, you know, right. Notice uh how these er mannerisms like this diminish your credibility, you know.

Tape record yourself presenting. Try to speak slowly and distinctly. Count the words you speak in 30 seconds. A comfortable and encouraging listening rate is two to three words per second. If you need to slow down, make yourself pause between sentences.

Relax before speaking. Take deep breaths, fill the diaphragm and exhale slowly. You will feel more relaxed and you'll better project your voice. Deep breathing also lowers your pitch, which makes you sound more credible.

Keep your throat lubricated by drinking plenty of water at room temperature.

ENHANCE YOUR STRENGTHS AND DIMINISH YOUR WEAKER POINTS. You provide the initial bolts of energy in the room. That's why it's important to connect with your audience. As you begin to talk, people will focus on your face.

Practice your expressions in the mirror. Also practice making eye contact. Practice the best walking and positioning patterns as you go through your content.

Videotape your run-through. Which mannerisms get in the way of your effectiveness? Eliminate distracting nervous gestures.

Give your entire presentation with visuals and any equipment you may use. Pay attention to the flow and timing. Notice any glitches that could translate into big problems.

Gather together a small friendly audience that will give you honest feedback.

Be timely. If you talk too briefly, people feel cheated. Too long and people get bored. Honor your audience by keeping to your time commitment.

SET THE STAGE FOR PRESENTATION PERFECTION

Elaine is speaking at her company's annual report presentation. This is her chance to shine in front of the shareholders and to present a positive image of her company. She's worked with several senior vice presidents on her speech and has a lively opening and planned presentation, complete with audience participation. The day of the speech, she intends to drop by the hotel conference room and check out everything, but she gets swamped with work.

"This is a first-class hotel," she thinks. "They'll have everything set up."

Perhaps the hotel's meeting planner had just ended a longtime relationship. Perhaps this planner was in such despair that work was merely dirt on the bottom of his shoes. That is the only way Elaine can explain the state of the room. The chairs are in straight rows. There are no tables. There is a huge podium in the front of the room, which comes up to Elaine's chin. There is no portable microphone. There is no screen set-up for the slides.

Elaine wants to pull her hair out.

THE ENVIRONMENT YOU'RE IN AFFECTS THE PRESENTATION.

Fast Fact
The tone of the room should reflect the size of the audience and the tone of your presentation.

Action
Check everything out before your presentation. Never take anything for granted.

MEETING ROOM PREPARATION

A safe and welcoming environment are essential to the success of your presentation. A few minutes checking out the set can spell the difference between success and failure.

1. Are you free to move away from the podium and out into the audience?

2. Are you limited to a hand-held mike or can you use a cordless, giving you greater mobility?

3. Who will be in the adjoining room?

4. Are there outside noises that can get in your way?

5. Is the room bright enough? Keep the lights to full capacity. When you turn down lights you turn down attention and retention.

6. If you're using an overhead projector slide, video or film, does the lighting wash out the screen? You may want to remove a bulb or reposition the screen or monitors.

7. Can everyone see you and your visuals? Before the group arrives, sit in various empty chairs and make sure.

8. Does the seating arrangement support the atmosphere you're creating? If you're informal, create a circle instead of straight rows of chairs. If you're creating a participatory workshop, use tables for a greater feeling of relaxation and comfort. You don't want obstacles between you and your audience. A small table at your side to hold notes is better than a lectern that hides you.

9. How is the temperature in the room? How do you control it?

10. Do you have drinking water readily available?

NINE TRICKS TO SPICY AND STYLISH PRESENTATIONS

As Erica leaves the board meeting, Jack stops her.

"I never laughed at a board meeting before. When you started that story about the lonely investor, I tell you, I was nervous. But they really ate it up."

AN ORIGINAL PRESENTATION WITH A SPLASH OF HUMOR ENLIVENS
YOUR AUDIENCE.

Fast Fact

Adults learn best when information is illustrated with humor and anecdotes.

Action

Any presentation benefits from your original thoughts laced with humor. Are you making the most of your natural abilities? Build an award-winning presentation with these tools and timbers:

1. *Be your own architect.* Design a speech that's original. Create your own stories and anecdotes. Avoid clichés and jargon.

2. *Cement your audience rapport* with sincerity, smiles and friendliness.

3. *Nail down your audience appeal.* Move toward the audience and make direct eye contact. Use gestures that include your audience and draw them in.

4. *Use your sense of interior design* to select clothes that give you calm and authority. Wear solid colors. These calm colors help you look more in control. Grays and blues command authority. Jewel colors, such as ruby red and emerald green, are power colors. Avoid large prints, floral or accessories that draw attention away from you and what you're saying.

5. *Use a checklist.* Before you go on stage, check your face, collar, make-up, shoulders for any distractions. Make sure your shoes are shined.

6. *Add humor to keep your presentation lively.* Adults learn best when they are having fun.

7. *Keep it clean.* Don't tell off-color jokes, or put-down stories.

8. *Paint a picture,* rather than teaching or preaching. Showing your audience rather than telling them gets them more involved. Use examples that illustrate your points.

9. *Know when it's time* to put down your tools and take a break. Take mental recesses. People learn in segments of 15 or 20 minutes, then you need to change directions and re-energize their interest.

HOW TO HANDLE A HECKLER

Bev is in the middle of her explanation of health care benefits when a guy in the back of the room says, "Yeah, we know how it works. We pour out our money and get nothing back."

Bev ignores him and continues with her flip chart.

"You insurance companies are all alike: crooks," he says.

Bev's mind is whirling. What should she do? How can she handle this guy? Isn't his supervisor somewhere in the audience? She wishes it were seventh grade, because then she could send him to the principal's office. But here, she's on her own. There's no supervisor and no principal.

DON'T TRY TO WIN OVER HOSTILE MEMBERS OF THE AUDIENCE.

Fast Fact
Protect yourself from hostile people. Don't give away your personal power to negative energy.

Action
Learn as much as possible about the hostile members in advance. Be prepared for their annoyance. Enjoy the receptive members of the audience and let them support you with their smiles, nods and eye contact.

Bev might use these techniques for dealing with this hostile man:

♦ Avoid eye contact.

♦ If he interrupts, respond with a "fogging" technique. Don't agree or accept, simply acknowledge his point of view by saying something benign, such as:

"I understand how you might see it that way."

"That's an interesting comment."

"I'll take that into consideration."

"I'd be happy to discuss it with you on break or following the presentation."

Or she might lighten the mood and acknowledge his jab by simply saying, "Ouch, that hurt," and move on.

THE FINALE: LEARN FROM YOUR EXPERIENCE AND BECOME A GREAT SPEAKER

At last, it's over. Even though her "Lunch and Learn" group is comprised of co-workers, Helen has been nervous about her presentation for weeks. She did it, it turned out OK and she doesn't want to ever think about it again.

EVALUATING YOUR PRESENTATION HELPS YOU BECOME A BETTER SPEAKER.

Fast Fact
Right after a speech is an ideal time to jot down what went right and what you'd like to change.

Action
First, congratulate yourself on your performance. Praise your bravery and your ability to get out here. Then, make a SPEAK SHEET that helps you analyze your speech.

- Make notes on what worked well.
- Write down moments when the audience seemed most with you and think about how you can expand on those for your next presentation.
- Did you accomplish your purpose?
- Did your audience stay with you?
- What could you have done better?
- Were there times you felt uncomfortable and why?
- Did you get your audience involved?

How to Use Your Self Profile to Improve Your Presentation Style

Susan loves talking in front of groups. She's full of interesting examples and stories and has no problem filling an hour or two. Sometimes, though, people walk out of her presentations wondering what she was really talking about.

Erin is crisp and to the point as a presenter. She whisks efficiently through the material, not loitering for examples or stories. "Everyone's busy," she says. "They don't have time for that touchy feely nonsense."

Lana really connects with her audience. She gets to know their needs beforehand and makes every presentation personable. Sometimes, though, she lets questions overwhelm her and loses control of the group.

Freida has every detail and every fact neatly laid out. She can recite them without looking at her notes and frowns if you interrupt her for questions. The details are everything to her and she doesn't tolerate frivolity.

Each quadrant of the SELF profile has its unique skills in the area of presentations.

Ss can count on their natural feeling of ease to win over groups. If you're an S, make sure you have a logical order and you stick with the purpose of your talk.

Es are brilliant at getting to the heart of things. If you're an E, relax, sprinkle in humor, ease up on the flood of information.

Ls feel really bonded to any group they present to. They instinctively understand what the group needs and are quick to let people participate. If you're an L, learn the difference between participation and interruption. Handle your interruptions quickly and gracefully.

Fs have all the facts, Ma'am. And then some. As an F, add some play and participation to keep your presentation effective.

No matter what your profile, speaking is a way to enhance your natural abilities and grow more competent and visible. Attend presentations and watch for style and effectiveness.

Now that you know the inside story on presentation, take the quiz again and see how you do.

Face the Facts About Presentations

1. You don't need presentation skills if you're just talking to your co-workers or your boss.　**True/False?**

2. You should never volunteer to speak.　**True/False?**

3. As a speaker, you can't control your audience's attention span.　**True/False?**

4. Using stories and anecdotes in your speech gets your audience off-track.　**True/False?**

5. Humor makes your presentation seem frivolous.　**True/False?**

6. Just standing in front of people makes them pay attention to everything you are saying.　**True/False?**

7. The best speeches are crammed with facts and details.　**True/False?**

8. You'll know when you've made it as a speaker: you'll be perfectly calm before each speech.　**True/False?**

9. If you know your subject well enough, you shouldn't have to practice your speech more than once.　**True/False?**

10. Gestures are nice but not necessary for your presentation.　**True/False?**

GRAND FINALE

You are practically ready to host your own talk show now. Mainly, you have the confidence and personal power to accept more speaking and presentation opportunities. You feel that by speaking out you're selling yourself. You've worked through the steps to powerful presentations and know that preparation is the key to success.

- You know that you have only thirty seconds to wow them with a first impression.
- You know that preparation is vital to being successful in speaking.

- Every detail is important. You've learned not to trust the experts, the maintenance crew, the meeting planner, but to check things out for yourself.
- You've learned the importance of a good opening.
- Analyzing your audience is one of the first ways you make your speech effective.
- You're taking up more space now, with your gestures, your voice and your stance, and therefore proclaiming more personal power.
- You know how to deal with interruptions.
- You know how to handle boredom and disinterest.
- You know that speaking improves your self-esteem, helps you learn and connects you with a lot of different people.
- You know that your SELF profile affects your speaking style.

CAPTURING WHAT YOU'VE LEARNED

Things I've learned

_____

_____

Concepts I want to try

_____

_____

Great ideas I want to share with others

_____

_____

Things I want to know more about

_____

_____

Chapter Ten

◇

IT'S NOT JUST WHAT YOU KNOW THAT COUNTS:
Mentoring and Networking

Ever wonder where your career might be if you had a mentor? Do you know how to find a mentor? What would you do if someone asked you to mentor them?

WHAT WOULD YOU ADVISE? TEST YOUR MENTORING SKILLS

Some of the most famous women in history met with a demise that might have been avoided, had they been successfully mentored. If you'd been their mentor, what advice would you have given these mythical women?

1. **Little Red Riding Hood.**

   a. Lift weights, Red. Stay in shape. You never know when you'll discover a wolf lurking around the corner.

   b. About this biscuit project, you might consider a stronger game plan. Spend less time chasing butterflies, be careful who you consult for advice, and clarify your goals to keep your focus.

   c. How many times must I tell you, "Don't share confidential information with wolves. You can't keep a secret to save your soul."

2. **Snow White.**

   a. Call the dwarfs and tell them it's been great, but you're moving on. More places to clean up, more men to nurture.

   b. Look, Snow, you've consulted seven people and they've all told you the queen's on a bum ride down the corporate ladder. You don't have to take everyone's advice, but seven in a row is a pretty strong clue.

   c. If you weren't such a codependent, you'd have a chance against the queen.

3. **Dorothy, the Wizard of Oz.**

   a. Look inside yourself for the answers, Dot. I mean, look at the team you've put together, a dude without a heart, and that wheat futures executive is brainless.

   b. What strength and determination you have! Sprinkle a little of that Oz creativity around the office, will you? How can we bring your whirlwind marketing trip a little closer to home and increase productivity?

   c. The road, Dorothy, is yellow, and brick. Stay on it. Every time I talk to you, you're off chasing another tin can.

4. **Cinderella.**

   a. Stay at it, Cindy. Plan your time, iron a little faster, and quit flirting with the mice upstairs. Then you can start giving time management seminars and dump the sisters completely.

b. Cut your losses. Use your network of friends to find another job.

c. It's hard all over, babe. Imagine what life would be like if you leaped on a prince's back and he locked you up in his castle.

5. **Beauty (and the Beast).**

a. In this world, you have to take care of yourself first. Go after the wicked fairy. Make her rescind the edict, and then deal one on one with the beast.

b. Weigh the odds, make a decision and stick with it. People go crazy when you keep changing your mind. You pulled yourself out of the mire, Beauty. You suffered defeat. Now listen to your instincts. Some of your resources come from unlikely places.

c. What a dreamer you are, always trying to make something gorgeous out of something dreadful. Why can't you see things the way they are?

6. **Sleeping Beauty.**

a. In case you haven't heard, your father prohibited spinning from a spindle. Buy woolen goods from department stores. Stay away from the big wheels.

b. You're in charge of your future. Don't be guided by another's predictions of who and what you should be. If you're getting bad advice, expand your network to include people who will help you succeed.

c. How convenient. I wish I could sleep for 100 years.

7. **Rapunzel.**

a. Alone again, eh Rap? Work late tonight. Fool the witch. Make her think you're taking over the castle. When she comes tomorrow, play on that fear.

b. Like many successful women, you feel alone now that you've reached the top. But if you'll look around, you'll find others like you who are on their way up, too. Women know other women's needs. Say what you need. Be specific.

   c. Doesn't that man give you a headache? I mean it's gross, disgusting. If he wants to reach the top, tell him to climb up someone else's hair.

SCORING

If you selected all As, you're trying to do it alone, which is traditional, outdated behavior for a woman. This chapter will show you why women need a mentor and how to find one.

If you selected all Bs, you're good at identifying the issues, you're serious about propelling your career, and you know the importance of relying upon others to get you there. You'll benefit the most from a successful relationship with a mentor. In fact, you might consider becoming a mentor. Women need more women mentors.

If you selected Cs, you're contributing to the downfall of women in business. Too often we criticize when we're really saying, "I wish I was at the top." We need to inspire and develop strategies that will help other women reach their goals. When we lift as we climb, we create a healthy, more productive and collaborative work environment.

In this chapter, you'll learn:

- Why it's important to have a mentor.
- How to get a mentor.
- What a mentor can do for you.
- How to make networking work for you.

If I Only Had a Mentor

Rebecca observes the players in her company. She's new and wants to make sure they notice her skills. At her previous job, she was a dependable leader in committee meetings, she followed through on assignments, yet she was frequently overlooked for promotions. This time she wants to make sure the "powers that be" notice her.

When she reviews the corporate telephone directory, she sees most of the people at the top are men.

"How does a woman in this company get noticed?" she asked.

MOVING UP THE LADDER ISN'T DETERMINED ONLY BY SKILL.

Fast Fact

People who make it to the top have at least one mentor from the "Powerful Group."

Action

Advancing your career is not solely dependent upon competence. You need to be recognized and groomed by those with positional power. People in positional power are those people who have made it to top-level positions.

White males have unlimited positional power. They can move in any direction; for them, there are no glass ceilings. They look the part, talk the part; they've established the rules and definition of positional power.

As a woman in business, you are under more scrutiny. You face more barriers, you have more roadblocks to overcome. Unless you have access to the "good old boys" club, you have less access to the inside scoop, and less information on how to "play the game."

"The male-dominated business environment does not validate the credibility of women in business," says Sally Jenkins, business consultant and trainer. "Find someone who's one of the chosen. Let their power rub off on you."

Mentors are important for a man to succeed and they're critical to a woman's success.

"With a mentor's support, you won't have to work as hard to prove yourself, and you'll take fewer pot shots," Jenkins says.

Set Goals Before You Look for a Mentor

Rebecca knows she needs a mentor. She goes up to the thirteenth floor where most executives have their offices and stops in the lounge to get a cup of coffee. She strolls past the tastefully decorated offices, and nods at the executives as she passes their offices.

A woman stops and asks, "Is there something I can do for you?"

"I'm new," Rebecca answers and introduces herself. "Human Resources gave me a tour last week, and I wanted to get a better feel for my work environment."

"Let me know if I can help," the woman answers. "My office is three doors down."

Rebecca realizes she's browsing like a shopper who doesn't exactly know what to purchase.

IDENTIFY YOUR GOALS BEFORE YOU SEEK A MENTOR.

Fast Fact

You'll select the best mentor when you know where you want to be two years from now.

Action

Make a personal goal list, then decide who will help you achieve your goals. The person you select as your mentor can make or break you in business. As you create your list, ask yourself some of these questions:

+ What position do I want?
+ If I achieve my professional goals, will they be compatible with the organization's goals?
+ Why did the organization hire me? How will my skills and resource network benefit the company?
+ Am I coachable? When someone gives me advice, do I let them know I'm taking the advice seriously? How do I respond to advice?
+ When I get advice, do people think I'm open and nonjudgmental?
+ Do I give people credit for seeing things I didn't see? For example, suppose you are fond of Krishna, a subordinate in your department, and you frequently favor her position in departmental issues. Jim, your boss, says Krishna's work isn't up to par, and that you need to challenge and motivate her, or transfer her to another department. Would you give Jim credit for seeing something you couldn't, even though Krishna is your favorite?

What a Mentor Can Do for You

The goal list was easy for Rebecca to create. As an independent woman, she excels at getting things done.

She leans back in her chair, sips coffee, and analyzes her list. She wonders if it's worth the hassle to find a mentor.

"Everything I've achieved, I've earned on my own," she says to herself. "I make car payments, house payments, I travel, I wear nice clothes. Why do I need a mentor?"

TOO OFTEN, WOMEN TRY TO GO IT ALONE. REMEMBER, THE POWERS THAT BE CAN PUT YOU IN TOUCH WITH THE RIGHT PEOPLE.

Fast Fact

Working with a mentor says these things about you:

- You're a team player.
- You understand the rules of the game.
- You're committed to learning the best skills in how to position yourself, how to connect and how to put your best self forward.

Action

If you're thinking of going it alone, think again. Here's what a mentor can do for you.

- A mentor helps you learn the ropes of the business. When she says, "The way we do things around here . . ." she's giving you information you won't find in the *Policies and Procedures* manual.
- A mentor serves as a sounding board for decisions and lets you know if you're on track.
- A mentor has keys to doors you can't open yourself.
- A mentor can help place you on the right projects that will increase your credibility and visibility.
- A mentor can be your voice at meetings you're not invited to attend. Once you've established a trusting relationship, your mentor can represent your ideas, keep you visible and give you credit when it matters.
- A mentor can recommend you for a promotion.

THE PROPER CARE AND NURTURING OF A MENTOR/PROTÉGÉE RELATIONSHIP

By now, Rebecca is convinced she needs a mentor. She's gregarious, she has a nice network of clients which she brought to the company, and she's good at motivating co-workers. After analyzing her goals, she realizes she'd like to be a division marketing manager within two years, and she'll need a mentor to help her make that goal. She examines the corporate structure and makes a list of potential mentors. Within the next two months, she plans to establish a mentor/protégée relationship.

FINDING THE RIGHT MENTOR/PROTÉGÉE MIX IS ONE OF THE BEST BUSINESS DECISIONS YOU'LL EVER MAKE.

Fast Fact

A strong mentor/protégée relationship depends on your careful research, knowing who's who in the organization, and a balance of give and take.

Action

People in large organizations have their own culture and they play their own political games. If you work for a large company, look inside to find your mentor.

People in small to midsize companies tend to run in cliques. You might be perceived as the "teacher's pet" and that destroys productivity. In this case, you might want to search for a mentor outside the company.

Mentors are especially valuable during the decade of buy-outs, mergers and acquisitions. Women with mentors outside the company already have an instant expert to turn to when job positions turn "iffy."

Steps to Creating a Winning Mentor/Protégée Relationship

STEP 1: SELECT THE CANDIDATES. Make a list of the powerful, influential and respected people in your organization. Then, turn into a researcher on a quest for knowledge. While you're in the coffee lounge, ask, "What do you know about the vice president of Marketing? What does the president think about him? How long has he been VP?" Ask similar questions about other candidates you've selected.

STEP 2: LET THEM GET TO KNOW YOU. Make yourself visible and begin building rapport with several people. A mentoring relationship happens; it cannot be forced. You'll want it to be mutually respectful.

♦ Take the initiative to begin conversations.

♦ Show up in the lounge when they're getting coffee.

♦ Invite the person to lunch with you.

STEP 3: ASK FOR WHAT YOU WANT. Use the direct approach and ask your mentor for help in reaching your goals. "I feel you have the skills and influence in this organization that I need to know about. I'd like to come to you for advice, talk to you about my goals. I know I can learn from you. And there are some things I can do for you. Will you mentor me?"

STEP 4: DEMONSTRATE YOUR COMMITMENT. If you reach mutual agreement, show your mentor you're fully committed to reaching your goals. This is crucial for women. Many men think women's lifestyles are changeable, and therefore that you're not committed to our goals. *Get help in your personal life to help back up your commitment. A man would do it. So should you.*

♦ Hire a nanny to care for the children, or discuss sharing parenting responsibilities with your spouse.

♦ Find a housesitter if you have to travel.

STEP 5: SPEAK FROM A POSITION OF STRENGTH. As you seek advice, avoid sounding helpless and deferring.

DON'T SAY: "I haven't a clue about this problem."

DO SAY: "This is the way I'm looking at it. And I would appreciate your input in how it may or may not work."

Respond to your mentor's advice with a brief thank you note and a sentence or two about how you followed up on it.

STEP 6: DEMONSTRATE RECIPROCITY. Make sure your mentor gets his or her needs met, too. Clarify from the beginning that this is a getting/giving relationship. You might offer to help out on special projects. You'll do your mentor a favor and you'll be seen by the "in" group. Make it a point to publicly give your mentor credit.

STEP 7: MALE MENTOR? CLARIFY RELATIONSHIP FROM THE START. Avoid any misunderstanding of sexual attraction or sexual innuendos. You might say, "I trust the fact that you're a man and I'm a woman won't get in the way of my learning from you." Use a few preventive measures to keep your relationship out of the rumor mills.

+ Make sure the door is open during your meetings.

+ Tell your grapevine about your mentor/protégée relationship. Feed them with information about how you enjoy working with a talented corporate leader. Always put your mentor in a good light. A businessman won't jeopardize his corporate position, especially if the person spreading good rumors says kind things about him.

STEP 8: LET THE RELATIONSHIP EVOLVE OVER TIME. Trust how you feel about the relationship. If you aren't growing or getting your needs met as you'd hoped, look elsewhere. If you sense your mentor is falling from power, be careful. You may topple with him. Know when it's time to change from a mentor/protégée relationship into one of equality, which is, after all, what you are striving to achieve. If you don't outgrow the relationship, you're sure to get stuck where you are.

How to Determine if the Relationship Is Working

For the last four months, Ramona and Tom have built a successful protégée/mentor relationship. She's been asked to serve on politically sensitive committees, she has a membership at the country club and frequently takes clients to lunch there. Tom freely gives her ideas, especially since Ramona often says, "Thanks for the compliment. Tom, my mentor, gave me several good suggestions."

Last week, Tom was tied up in two huge projects which Ramona could have helped him with if he'd asked for help.

She wonders if she's giving enough back to the relationship. Is she taking too much? Does he think it's time for her to move on? These are questions she needs to check out with him.

THE BEST MENTOR/PROTÉGÉE RELATIONSHIPS ARE NEVER FORCED.

Fast Fact

Mentor/protégée relationships work like the dynamics of a friendship where people give and get to keep the relationship in balance.

Action

A good mentoring relationship is synergistic. Your mentor is rewarded by watching your growth, similar to a parent/child relationship. Successful parents are rewarded when the child grows and develops, and eventually stands on her own two feet.

The bottom line is, the workplace is more productive when the relationship works.

If you're like Ramona, you've been taught to be self-contained, thinking that the only way to get something done is to do it yourself. The mentor/protégée relationship is your key to advancing your career, and if it's working, some of these things will happen:

+ Your knowledge will grow.

+ Your personal and positional power will increase.

+ Knowing someone at the top has faith in you lets you have more faith in yourself and take more risks.

+ People will notice your work.

+ Your mentor will hear that you've given him credit for the ideas you use.

+ Your mentor will represent you at meetings you're not invited to attend and give you credit for the ideas.

+ You and your mentor will share new contacts.

HOW TO CHANGE FROM MENTOR/PROTÉGÉE TO EQUAL

For several weeks, Ramona heard complaints about glitches in the company's accounting software. Since these glitches affect her department's productivity, Ramona wants to compare the cost of an on-staff computer programmer against the cost of new software.

"I'd like to bounce an idea off you," Ramona says when she's in Tom's office.

He listens, gives her feedback and like other conversations, suggests names of people she should interview.

Ramona writes down the names, then says, "I'd like to chair this committee. You've given me a tremendous boost, and I'd like to keep coming to you with ideas. Right now, I believe I have the skills to help the committee make the right decision."

"By all means," Tom says. "Let me know any time you need my help."

WHEN YOU FEEL YOU CAN MAKE IT ON YOUR OWN, IT'S TIME TO CHANGE THE RELATIONSHIP TO ONE OF EQUALITY.

Fast Fact

You have the most to gain by taking control of your career development.

Action

There's an old saying: Give someone a fish and she eats for a day. Teach her how to fish and she eats for a lifetime.

Your mentor will always be a significant person in your career development. If you don't outgrow the relationship, you're sure to be stuck in middle management. Trust your instincts to tell you when it's time to change or move into a position of equality. Here are some ways you'll know when the relationship should change.

♦ You'll feel like you can make it on your own.

♦ You'll stop asking for as much help.

♦ You'll feel like you're no longer growing in the relationship.

♦ You'll depend upon the friendships you've developed and your networking skills.

SHOULD YOU BE A MENTOR?

As a mentor, people turn to you to help them make changes and offer advice. You become a mentor because you've earned the right to mentor. You've developed knowledge, you've jumped through hoops, paid your dues, learned the political ropes.

Up until the 1990s, women have relied on men to be their mentors. In most cases, this was not by choice but by the design of the system. Positions at the top have been, and still are, highly populated by men.

WOMEN NEED SUCCESSFUL WOMEN AS ROLE MODELS AND MENTORS.

Fast Fact
Women are by nature successful at mentoring.

Action
There's never been a better time for women to mentor, and there's never been a greater need for women mentors.

Women as leaders will make the organization a more human place to work. Consider making yourself available as a mentor using these guidelines.

1. Seek out opportunities to mentor other women. When any one of us looks good, we all look good.
2. Avoid the "Queen Bee" mentality. A QB is someone who carries these thoughts:
   - I'm no longer one of the girls.
   - I pulled myself up by my boot straps, and so can you.
   - A QB isolates herself.
3. The good of the company and the people in it are your Number One concern. Be careful so management doesn't wonder "Whose side is she on?" Is she here for the company, or is she here to help women get ahead? The two should not be exclusive of each other.

THE SECRET OF EFFECTIVE NETWORKING

Betsy arrives at the luncheon, checks in at the reservation table and hangs her name tag on her right lapel. Once inside, she realizes there are more than 100 women like her getting to know each other. As a new member to the professional group, she's determined to do some networking.

Immediately, she's relieved when a client greets her.

"How are you?" the client asks.

"Not bad," Betsy answers.

"What's new?" the client asks.

"Not much," Betsy says. She senses the people around her know more about networking than she does, and she's missing business opportunities. She and the client agree they need to get together some time and Betsy moves on. Her main goal is to get through the luncheon, gather business cards from as many women as she can, and safely return to her desk.

Betsy suffers from the "good girl" syndrome. She's content to be nice, and hopes that if she's good at what she does, the rewards will follow.

USE THE SKILLS OF EFFECTIVE NETWORKING TO INCREASE YOUR VISIBILITY AND STRENGTHEN YOUR CAREER.

Fast Fact

86% of jobs are found through networking. Only 5% of available jobs are in the newspaper. You'll have seven different jobs in your work life. Only three of those will be voluntary changes.

Action

"Women have a mistaken notion about networking," says Anne Baber, co-author, *Great Connections: Small Talk and Networking for Businesspeople* (Impact Publications, 1992). "They network for what they can get. Focus on what you can give. You can't control what you get, you can only control what you give."

Start creating your support network while you're employed. Networking isn't an event, it's a process, and it takes at least six months of concentrated effort to build. The worst time to build a network is when you're out of a job.

As you prepare for a gathering of professionals, focus on what you have to give, then on what you want to get.

- Make a list or agenda of what you're looking for. Begin with something important to you, such as where to find silk boxer shorts or a silver ladle for holiday presents. This opens conversations and gives people a reason to want to help you.
- Ask yourself, "What makes me enthusiastic?" Take every opportunity to demonstrate your capabilities. Get active in the group. Get visible.

- Make yourself approachable. Do this by first being a giver. Return phone calls. Use your network to connect resources if someone needs help.
- Ask for business cards.

Whether you're networking with co-workers or colleagues, you're building a personal team of experts who will be available for you when you need them. Here's what you can do:

- Join organizations related to your field. Be an active member to let others recognize your abilities. Attend meetings, get to know the officers, offer to do small tasks for the organization that will get your name in print.

- Be selective of the additional activities you take on. Make sure they are the "right ones" that position you with increased credibility and visibility.

- If you agree to a task, under-promise, then over-deliver. Women tend to take on too much, to over-promise. You'll spread your time and energy too thin, causing you to under-deliver.

- Take colleagues to breakfast or lunch. Let them talk about themselves. You'll sound brilliant if you let them talk first. Tell them what you're doing. Ask for contacts. File these alphabetically or by categories of information.

- Refer colleagues to conferences. Send them copies of articles. Your colleagues like knowing you're keeping them in mind, plus they'll think of you when they need someone on their team.

- Offer to teach a class at a college or university. If you're looking for support, you'll find new professional friends.

How to's of Networking: What to Do, What to Say

Chantelle believes she's a well-organized business woman at work. She likes the comfort of her own space, and is gregarious with those she works with. But when she gets into crowds, she tends to freeze up. She doesn't know what to say, she's not sure how to introduce herself. This frustrates her because she knows she needs to network.

NETWORKING IS LIKE BREATHING. IT'S A NATURAL SKILL FOR WOMEN. WE DO IT ALL THE TIME, YET WE HESITATE TO GIVE OURSELVES CREDIT FOR IT.

Fast Fact

If you tell people what you want, they'll help you get it.

Action

The main rule in networking is, "Be interested in people and they will be interested in you."

When Baber counsels people in networking, she encourages them to practice the **Four Es.**

- ♦ **Enjoy** the moment. Networking is making the most of small talk.

- ♦ **Engage** in a satisfying relationship with each other. Get beyond the superficial routines.

- ♦ **Exchange** valuable information. Put up your antennae. Be aware of what the speaker is looking for. Ask probing questions to know their challenges. Give information, then get some in return. Know what information you're looking for.

- ♦ **Explore** future opportunities. Develop a good relationship for the future. Networking isn't the time for either of you to get deep into a project. Make an appointment for breakfast or lunch to focus on opportunities.

Networking is a subtle form of doing business. It's different from friendships and it's different from marketing. To make networking work for you, follow these 10 steps.

Step 1 Be prepared before each professional meeting. Know what you have to offer, and know what you want to get.

Step 2 Make sure you know your audience. Is it comprised of mostly men or women? Do the members share your level of experience, or is their experience in other fields? Will you be making new contacts or renewing former ones?

Step 3 When you arrive, take the initiative to introduce yourself. Prepare an introduction. Women seldom say enough about themselves. Too often women introduce themselves as a "just a." "I'm just a secretary," or "I'm just an office manager." Describe what you do. Position yourself with credibility. Put yourself in the best light.

Don't say: "Hello, I'm Betty Smith."

Do say: "Hello, I'm Betty Smith. I work at First National Bank. I've been there for 7 years and I manage the commercial accounts."

Step 4 Make yourself approachable. Do this with open body language.

Step 5 Take the initiative to shake hands. Grasp the person's hand firmly. Shake once, twice from the elbow up and down. If the person gives you a wimpy handshake, slightly touch your forehand over theirs and move in web to web.

Step 6 Exchange business cards. Keep them in your pocket where they're easily reachable to avoid the clumsiness of searching through your purse or brief case. Put a note on the back of their card to remind you about this person's skills, and write the date. When you return to your office, file the cards by categories.

Step 7 Master small talk and keep moving. In a gathering, expect to spend 5–7 minutes with each person. Tell them you hope to get a chance to visit with them again before the lunch or evening is over.

Step 8 Extend yourself. If you can do someone a favor, do it.

Step 9 Follow up if you think the contact is important to you. Offer to take the person to lunch. Write a note, and tell the contact it was a pleasure meeting her.

Step 10 Stay visible. When someone within your network receives recognition, call and congratulate them or drop a note.

GRAND TOTALS

- A mentor will help you learn the political ropes, enabling you at times to short circuit problem areas.

- A mentor will give you the necessary feedback on your performance to help you advance your career.

- The mentor/protégée relationship cannot be forced. To make it work, both parties need to receive something in return.

- A mentor will represent your ideas and go to bat for you when the going gets tough.

- Advancing your career is not completely dependent upon skill. It also depends on who you know and who knows you.

- A mentor can make or break your career.

- If your mentor falls from power, be careful. You may slip, too.

- Expect to outgrow the relationship or you may be stuck in your present position.

- Women need more strong women mentors. If one looks good, we all look good.

- Networking is the key to making effective business contacts work for you.

CAPTURING WHAT YOU'VE LEARNED

Things I've learned

_____

_____

Concepts I want to try

_____

_____

Great ideas I want to share with others

_____

_____

Things I want to know more about

_____

_____

Chapter Eleven

◇

YOUR PERSONAL POWER AND CONFRONTING SEXUAL HARASSMENT

Sexual harassment is not about sex. It's about power. If you think you're being sexually harassed, seek legal counsel. This chapter, however, is not about legal advice. Rather, it's about empowerment. You'll learn the definition of sexual harassment, learn what to do or say when it happens to you, and empower yourself to significantly reduce the chance that it will happen to you.

TEST YOURSELF: WHAT WOULD YOU DO?

1. You're driving home from work. Traffic on the interstate finally breaks loose and you speed up. A sleek silver Cadillac pulls up beside you and intentionally runs even with you. You speed

up. So does the Cadillac. You slow down. The Cadillac slows also. You become anxious, feeling threatened by the car's presence. You look into the next lane and notice the driver is a co-worker. He smiles and waves. What do you do?

a. Smile weakly in return. Wave sheepishly. How silly of you to think someone would try to harm you.

b. Speak poorly of his ancestry. Speed up, cut him off, then slam on your brakes. Anyone trying to make a fool out of you deserves to lose his front end.

c. Look at him. Don't smile, don't wave. Tomorrow when you see him, say, "I don't think automobiles are an appropriate power tool for the road. If you need my attention, let's talk about it while we're still at work."

2. You're working at the computer when you see a man standing beside you. You look up. Like always, Ray hovers over you. His belt loop is stretched, he's popped another shirt button, but he's so close, you can hardly focus to see his face. What do you do?

a. Scoot your chair back. When he comes closer, scoot back again.

b. Remove your letter opener from your desk drawer and pop the other buttons on his shirt.

c. Say, "Ray, I can't see you, and I feel uncomfortable when you're this close. Please back away from me."

3. Theodore has been the company's CFO since 1950. He is the nicest man, loves his family and jokes around with everyone in the office. When you started as an accountant last year, everyone called him "Uncle Teddy" because he's such a touchy-feely man. He used to give you little hugs, but lately he's been kissing your cheek. Today, when you give him the monthly financial statement, he tries to kiss you on the mouth. "You're not afraid of me?" he says when you resist. You

a. Say, "Of course I'm not. I'm just in a bad mood."

b. Tighten the knot on his tie until his face turns blue. Ask him if anyone in his family wants to know how much he spent last year on personal entertainment.

    c. Say, "Theodore, I recognize you as an important person in this company and I don't like to be touched like this."

4. Your boyfriend drives you to work and gives you a kiss as you leave the car. Inside the office, Brian, a male co-worker, joins you as you're walking to your desk. He says, "Long night, eh? Bet you're one hell of a pussycat." You say, "My private life is none of your business, Brian." Brian says, "Ooooh! Guess who didn't get much sleep." What do you do?

    a. Laugh gingerly. Tell yourself Brian's trying to be friendly. Besides, he's a man with power around this place. Try to be nice to him.

    b. Slam your purse into his belly. When Brian laughs again, call your boyfriend and say, "Honey, there's this bully at work who's always trying to put his hands on me. Can you make him stop?"

    c. Stop and look directly at Brian. Say, "I consider your comments to be sexually harassing and I don't want you to talk to me like that again." When you get back to your desk, write a letter describing Brian's behavior and give him a copy of the letter. Tell him if he harasses you again, you'll send a copy of the letter to his boss.

5. As a continuing education director, you bring guest speakers to the college from all over the country. A male speaker comes highly recommended to you from several sources. You outline your expectations with him before he arrives. During the conference, a student files a sexual harassment report against him. What do you do?

    a. Accept the report. File it in your private records. Say to the student, "I know this person very well and this is not consistent with his behavior. Can you tell me what provoked him?"

    b. Invite the speaker into your office. Say, "You came to us highly recommended, and I don't know what's going on. Sexual harassment will not be tolerated on our campus. You'll have to leave."

c. Accept the report. Tell the student you're scheduling a private conference and the three of you will discuss the event which caused her to file. Tell her you plan to take the claim down to Human Resources and you'll ask both the student and speaker to comment and sign an affidavit.

6. You're an interior designer on a two-hour flight to meet with clients in Milwaukee. During the flight, you strike up a conversation with Ryan, a vice-president of marketing. As a matter of fact, his company is relocating and needs a design consultant for their new offices. You meet him in the lobby of your hotel and have dinner in the restaurant. Ryan is an attentive listener. After the meal, he says, "You're a gorgeous woman. I'd like to get to know you better. Why don't we tidy up this contract in your room? I'll have a bottle of brandy sent up and when we're both comfortable, we can agree on the terms of your project." What do you do?

a. Here you are in Milwaukee with an attentive listener. You know how hard it is to find a man who listens these days? Smile coyly. After all, you're sure he'll keep his word.

b. Slap his face. Say, "Do I look like a hooker? You guys are all alike." Pour water down his shirt, catch the first elevator back to your room.

c. Say, "A brandy would be fine, and I'd like to share it with you right here in the restaurant. I can meet with you tomorrow morning at 9:00 A.M. so we can design a contract that meets both our needs."

7. During the last two to three months, you've been dieting. Sometimes the pounds come off easily. Sometimes they don't. You come into the coffee lounge and face a plate of chocolate-and-caramel-swirled brownies. Adam is also there. Ever since you started the diet, he repeatedly comments on your state of thinness. He sees you drool over the plate and says, "If you eat that stuff, you'll get fat and sassy. Of course, you're already . . . sassy." What do you do?

a. Rush out of the lounge and hide in your office. Call the gym and reactivate your membership. Buy another diet book, swear you'll eat rice for the next year.

    b. Say, "Look, Cueball, I guess you're probably not blinding the office with your neon headpiece. Who died and left you prince of weight control?"

    c. Say, "Adam, I find your comments offensive. We have to work together and I don't want rude remarks to get in the way of my productivity. Please don't make comments about my body again."

8. When you joined the company, you found a mentor who helped you move up the corporate ladder. Now you're vice-president of sales, you frequently work overtime, and predominantly with men because there are few women at your level. On your way to the office, you overhear a male junior executive say, "Now that she's this far, I wonder who's left for her to sleep with." What do you do?

    a. Let him sneer. Ignorance runs rampant among youth.

    b. Send a memo to his supervisor. Tell the supervisor you're unhappy with the man's work, you think he might be better suited for another agency. Stay at it until the man comes to his senses or leaves the company.

    c. Step into the young man's office. Say, "I consider your comment about my sleeping arrangements to be sexually harassing. You can get ahead in this office by supporting your co-workers, not by discrediting them. That's how we maintain high productivity here. I want those comments stopped."

9. You're at a sophisticated banquet. There are ten people at your table; one person is telling raunchy jokes filled with four-letter words and trashy sexual scenes. He pauses to pour another glass of wine. What do you do?

    a. Look away from him. Ignore him. He'll get the message.

    b. Grab the wine bottle from him. Say, "I think you've had enough for tonight." When he bellows at you, gag him with your napkin.

    c. Say, "Perhaps those jokes were inappropriate. They were offensive to me. Please don't talk like that in front of me again."

10. You come to work and there's a videotape on your desk. When you play it, you discover it's a tape of several women's body parts, including yours. What do you do?

    a. Rush around the office and confiscate all the copies. Buy new clothes. Change your hair.

    b. Stand outside the office and demand to know who filmed the videotape.

    c. Take the tape to Human Resources. Include a memo and give details about where you found it, what's on it, and what you'd like Human Resources to do about it. Keep a copy of your memo in your office.

SCORING

If you answered mostly As, you have a hard time defining your personal limits. Your low self-esteem gets in the way of your right to be treated with respect. If you allow harassing statements or sexual innuendos, you relinquish your power to someone else. You're giving others the power to box you in. They define who you are and what you can do. Reread the chapter on self-esteem. Then, use this chapter to help you put an end to sexually harassing incidents.

If you answered mostly Bs, you're dealing with strong anger issues toward men. You may even have had good cause, but getting even isn't the answer. Talking directly to the abuser or harasser is the key to empowerment. This chapter will help you define your limits and appropriately express your anger so that you don't fall into the same behavior as the harasser.

If you answered mostly Cs, you have a strong sense of your limits. People around you understand what is and what is not acceptable behavior.

EMPOWER YOURSELF BY WORKING WITH OTHERS TO CHANGE ATTITUDES

Retraining is the foundation to change.

At a luncheon, MaryEllen complains about the rampant sexual abuse in her office. "It comes at us women from every direction. It seems to be condoned from the top down. There are no women at the top to make a stand. No one listens to the women, we're just the support staff. We're just the ones who keep this company running. It's hopeless. Men aren't going to change. I either have to put up with it, or leave the company."

Freida listens empathically to MaryEllen's frustrations. Other women share their harassing stories. As a workshop leader, Freida knows the women need to get rid of their frustrations before she can start a paradigm shift and turn their ideas around.

"Think about what MADD has done by acting as a collective force," Freida says. "Jokes about drunks aren't funny any more."

WOMEN WORKING COLLECTIVELY CAN ELIMINATE SEXUAL HARASSMENT FROM THE WORKPLACE.

Fast Fact
One voice will be heard. It takes a thousand voices to create change.

Action
Sexual harassment is any explicit demeaning sexual behavior, including physical and verbal, that is unwanted and unwelcome by the victim. Some types of harassment include:

- Unwanted and inappropriate touching.
- Unwelcome hugs and kisses.
- Consistent invasion of space.
- Propositions.
- Sexual innuendoes.
- Lewd comments.
- A promise or threat in exchange for sex.
- Repeated dirty jokes.
- Repeated comments about physical appearance.

Source: EEOC Sexual Harassment Guidelines

How Much Do You Know About Sexual Harassment?

Write an A if you agree with the following commonly-held ideas about sexual harassment issues. If you disagree, write a D.

——— 1. Women in blue collar jobs are more likely to be sexually harassed than professional women.

——— 2. More women harass men today than 10 years ago.

——— 3. If a woman dresses in clothes that show she has positional power, she will not be sexually harassed at work.

——— 4. With today's media coverage, more women are filing false charges of harassment.

——— 5. An employer is only liable if a superior sexually harasses a subordinate. The employer is not liable for harassment between co-workers.

——— 6. Women who are the first to enter nontraditional jobs, which are historically for male workers, will experience the most sexual harassment.

——— 7. Mild behaviors such as flirting and off-color jokes do not constitute harassment.

——— 8. A woman who says "No" discourages anyone from harassing her.

——— 9. A good manager knows when there is harassment in his or her department.

———10. Members of the same sex can be involved in harassment.

———11. A woman can file a sexual harassment suit if someone refuses to hire her because of her gender.

———12. A woman who is tactful and has strong people skills can easily handle unwanted sexual advances at work.

Answers:

Disagree with all, except #6.

What Men Don't Know Can Harm You

"I'd better not catch anyone treating my daughters like women around here are treated," says 45-year-old Danny who keeps photos of his daughters on his desk. "By the time my kids are grown, this might be a decent place to work."

Danny's office politics give a contradicting message. He keeps "girlie" magazines in his credenza, he arrives at meetings early and shares raw cartoons with the guys.

He and his last secretary, Debbie, frequently went out for drinks with friends after work. She called him "honey" and he called her "toots." One day, Debbie was suddenly unemployed and Danny got a new secretary.

Mattie, his new administrative assistant, dresses in business clothes, she networks with other professional women and she's gradually educating Danny to treat her respectfully.

"My name's Mattie," she says, when he tries "toots" on her. "And I'd like to be called by my name."

"I don't understand her. Sometimes I think she's trying to force me out of my job," Danny says. "I thought if I showed her these silly cartoons, she'd warm up to me."

Mattie says, "These pictures don't do anything for me, and your showing them to me interferes with my productivity. I'd like to make this a decent place to work."

REMOVING SEXUAL HARASSMENT FROM THE WORKPLACE IS AN EDUCATIONAL PROCESS.

Fast Fact
85% of sexual harassment comes from people who are unaware that what they are doing is harmful.

Action
You can be conservatively dressed, talk powerfully, walk with power, and still be harassed. Harassment is about power, the kind of power that fears the unknown. Educating co-workers helps eliminate the unknown and resulting power struggle.

Most men try to understand women through traditional roles. They feel more comfortable dealing with a woman as a mother, wife, lover or daughter, and not as an equal.

Traditionally, men build their self-esteem around work, actions, achievements, accomplishments, and decisions. Women build self-esteem around the quality of relationships. To be treated as an equal, combine the esteem that you gain from your work ethic and meaningful relationships.

When educating your male counterparts about equality, be professional and maintain a business relationship. Be assertive in letting them know what specific behaviors are unwanted and unwelcome.

Project a powerful image as you build relationships with men. You don't need to be 5 foot 11 inches and have a black belt to do this. When people meet Anne for the first time, they are always surprised at how short she is.

"I thought you were at least six feet tall," people say. "You have a determined attitude, like you can handle anything."

Be consistent in how you walk, talk, and dress. Be clear about your professional image and be consistent in teaching people how to treat you.

Commanding respect and educating co-workers was a huge challenge for the first woman in a nontraditional job. Consider some of the following fields where women educated men about sexual harassment issues. Today these pioneer women have paved the path for other women.

First female crew member on an airline.

First female surgeon.

First female attorney.

First female mail carrier.

First female fire fighter.

Women experienced more sexual harassment than the

First male flight attendant.

First male secretary.

First male dental hygienist.

First male nurse.

How to Handle the Three Types of Harassers

Researchers who studied sexual harassment among these firsts have identified three types of harassers.

1. UNAWARE HARASSER. Eighty-five percent of harassers are simply unaware that their behavior is offensive or unwanted. These co-workers respond well when you set your limits and identify what is appropriate and what is not appropriate.

2. DELIBERATE HARASSER. These people know their behavior is harmful and unwanted, but they are testing the boundaries, as if to ask, "How much can I get away with?"

They keep harassing because they're certain your response will be predictable. If you work with someone in this category, you'll have to take stronger action to eliminate harassment in your office. Most likely, they've been getting away with harassment for several years. Women need to bond together to take a stand against a deliberate harasser.

An interesting analogy to the deliberate harasser is the relationship between an alcoholic and the spouse. In alcoholic relationships, women are often the caretakers and nurturers who believe it's their responsibility to take care of the offender.

A recent study presented by Betty Ford revealed amazing results. Out of 10 situations where the man was the alcoholic, nine women stayed in the marriage. Only one had enough self-esteem to remove herself. When the woman was the alcoholic, nine men left the marriage, and only one man felt obligated to stay.

3. UNCONTROLLABLE HARASSER. People in this category are psychologically disturbed. They can't control their harassing behavior. An uncontrollable harasser needs professional help. If you think you're working with an uncontrollable harasser, get Human Resources involved immediately. No company worth its salt can afford to accommodate a harasser, particularly now with so many sexual harassment suits brought to court.

THE EDUCATION PROCESS

Joanna is a business education administrator at a sophisticated community college which serves more than 500 area clients. She is a superb listener, an articulate speaker and frequently gives communication seminars.

Bob, the Dean of Business and Industry, raved about her professionalism and encouraged her to take this position. He's been with the college for twenty years, is tenured and considers himself a jovial member of the administration.

As Joanna arrives at her office, Bob jabs his elbow into her side and teases, "Joanna, are you wearing a push-up bra? You're looking a little chestier today."

Joanna studies him and says, "Excuse me, Bob, I want to make sure I heard what you said. Did you say, 'Are you wearing a push-up bra? You're looking a little chestier today?'"

Bob hears what he says and immediately apologizes. "I guess that sounded rather stupid, didn't it?"

YOU HAVE THE AWESOME RESPONSIBILITY FOR YOUR OWN REACTIONS TO THE SITUATIONS IN YOUR LIFE.

Fast Fact

Preparation + Practice = Spontaneous Response—*Sue Carnahan,* President, Carnahan & Associates Training and Consulting

Action

"What you know and what you believe are two different notions," says Sue Carnahan, President. "Your self-esteem and self-worth are tied up in your belief systems. Believe that you are worthy of being treated respectfully."

Know the difference between sexual energy and sexual harassment. "Sexual energy in the workplace is productive and energizing," Carnahan says. "Repeated unwanted sexual comments or actions is sexual harassment, and it interferes with productivity.

"If the conversation takes a wrong turn, it's up to you to get it back in the right direction."

Five-Point Empowerment Checklist

In their training sessions, Carnahan and Kay Keller use a Five-Point Checklist that empowers women to take control.

1. *Listen. Don't overreact.* Keep your mind on the words. This helps you focus on your response, not on the person.
2. *Repeat the statement.* Repeat as closely as possible what you think you heard. "Bob, did I hear you ask me if I was wearing a

push-up bra today?" Usually the speaker recoils when he hears his words replayed.

3. *Clarification.* Clarify the remark by asking a question. "I'm puzzled, Bob. What is it about my clothing that has anything to do with my job?" Or, "I'm puzzled, Bob. What is it about our work relationship that makes you think I want to have an affair?"

4. *Write down word for word what the person has said.* "I think you're making an interesting statement, Bob. I want to make sure I get this down." Start jotting Bob's comments, read them aloud as you write.

5. *Set limits.* Say, "I don't appreciate your remarks." Or, "I don't want you to talk to me like that." Or, "Keep your hands off me. This relationship is strictly business. Do you understand?" By adding the "Do You Understand?" you force the person to stand accountable for his or her decision.

You feel victimized when you've lost control. If you have no choices, you have no control. You might feel out of control if

- ♦ You're afraid you'll fail a class because a professor makes unwanted passes at you.
- ♦ You fear you'll lose your job if you stand up to your boss's advances.
- ♦ You feel nauseous when a harasser is in your presence.

You can empower yourself using the "Broken Record" technique many parents use with their children. Be careful that you don't lose power and have to rebuild.

Mom: Johnny, pick up your room before you watch TV.

Johnny: Oh, Mom, I can't get it done before my show's on.

Mom: Johnny, pick up your room before you watch TV.

Johnny: But Mom, this is my favorite show and I can't miss it again this week.

Mom: Johnny, pick up your room before you watch TV.

Johnny: If you let me watch this one show, I'll clean up my room and I'll do the dishes.

Mom: Well, all right.

The mom here lost her power and when the show's over, she'll have to build it again. To maintain her power, Mom needs to say:

Mom: The subject is non-negotiable. Pick up your room before you watch TV.

Mom's conversation is an example of the "Broken Record" technique. Use the same technique with the sexual harasser. The message gets through when you state your limits often enough and strong enough.

The Broken Record

Bob: But I call everybody sweetie. It doesn't bother anyone else.

You: I am uncomfortable when you call me sweetie. Please call me by my name. (Say the same thing several times and Bob will get the message.)

The sexual harasser uses the "Fogging Technique" to avoid the issue. In the example below, Bob is clouding, or fogging, the harassment issue.

Fogging Technique

You: Bob, my name is Mary. I'd like to be called by my name.

Bob: Oooh, aren't you sensitive.

You: I may be sensitive sometimes and I still want to be called by my name. (This takes the focus off the unrelated issue and places it back on the real issue.)

The Subject Is Not . . .

Bob: Oooh, didn't we wake up on the wrong side of the bed.

You: The subject is not about my sleep. The subject is I want to be called by my name.

HOW TO CREATE AN HONORABLE, SAFE WORKPLACE

After five jobs and three different cities, Magdala is finally pulling many decades of cultural, religious and family history into one nicely packaged woman.

She was raised in a conservative religious decade when the first float in Eisenhower's inaugural parade was a float to God. At nineteen, she dressed in bell-bottoms, braided her hair and rebelled against the establishment. During the seventies and eighties, she accepted odd job titles and transfers to move up the corporate ladder, frequently negotiating her way in and out of sexually harassing situations.

When she was promoted to Regional Director, she felt at last she wouldn't have to set limits about sexual issues.

While she talks to the president of the company at a sophisticated dinner party, another Regional Director grabs her from behind and whispers sexual innuendos in her ear. Magdala happens to know this Regional Director wants to take over Magdala's region.

"Excuse me," Magdala says to her colleague. "This company honors their employees. I think what you said is inappropriate."

EDUCATION CREATES A SAFE, HONORABLE PLACE TO WORK.

Fast Fact

Harassment is not about *intent.* It's about impact on the individual.

Action

"As the workplace changes with regard to cultural make-up, gender make-up and generational differences, we need to establish and learn new ways to relate to each other," says Sherri Cannon, international trainer and consultant.

"You can't depend on traditional ways to work together. You need to create an honorable and safe place for everyone."

You deserve to work in a safe place where you are respected. For some men, this means giving up the fun of "pillow talk" or discounting language. When you respond assertively, be prepared for a comeback. Perhaps you work with someone who refers to people in his office as his "girls" or "sweetie." Repeat your lines until you're prepared and confident in delivering them.

Maintain Your Privacy

Be cautious about revealing your private life at work. Keep your business life strictly professional and separate from your social life.

Use the **Platinum Rule** as a simple guideline.

TREAT OTHERS AS THEY WANT TO BE TREATED.

If someone extends a hand to be shaken, shake it. Don't hug instead.

In some regions of the country, some men may feel it's appropriate to greet a woman by kissing her on the cheek in place of a handshake. If this makes you uncomfortable, extend your hand as you say, "Mr. Smith, I'd like to shake your hand."

Dating at work is risky business. If someone learns about a liasion you're having with a man, you'll most likely become the sacrifice. Your professional and private reputation may be permanently damaged, or career derailed.

One seemingly harmless example is in a previous case where Danny and Debbie, his secretary, frequented bars with friends after work. Danny and Debbie were never sexually involved, but since they used "pillow" language, they were getting credit for sleeping together. They worked in a male-dominated industry, so while Danny was placed on two-weeks probation, Debbie found herself out on the streets looking for a new job.

Many companies still tend to blame the woman. After all, she is usually in the subordinate position. Corporations that don't have a written policy on office dating are usually making a big mistake. Anything that threatens the integrity of the workplace should be forbidden.

If you're working without such a policy, here are some guidelines to follow:

1. Any office affair that causes employees to complain or gossip will not be tolerated.

2. If an inside relationship exists, the manager will discuss the affair with the individuals involved, let them know they are in direct violation of company policy and the affair must end. If they do not wish to end the relationship, one person must elect to be transferred or leave the company.

3. If the affair comes to an end, the manager should discuss transfer or buy-out options to avoid further problems.

WHAT TO DO IF YOU'RE SEXUALLY HARASSED

Carole works in an office with Gil, a deliberate harasser who constantly affronts her about her weight and breast size. She wears clothes that conceal her breasts, but Gil brushes against her. "I can't see your Jane Russells today. I love those tits," he says. "Don't hide them from me."

"Why won't you stand up to him?" her co-worker asks.

"I need my job," Carole answers.

"He's getting away with this because he knows how you'll respond. Why don't you do something totally unpredictable?"

"I'd like to shove his false teeth down his throat."

"If he's doing it to you, he's done it to others," the friend says. "You've got to be the first to stand up to him. You're strong enough to do it."

YOU HAVE A RIGHT TO DEFEND YOURSELF.

Fast Fact

An employer is responsible for acts of sexual harassment in the workplace where the employer knows or should have known of the conduct, unless it can show that it took immediate and appropriate corrective action.—*EEOC Sexual Harassment Guidelines*

Action

If you've used the Five-Point Checklist and the harasser continues unwanted behavior, it's time to take written action.

1. Put the unwanted and unwelcome behaviors in writing. Send a carbon copy to your boss, and keep a copy in your files.
2. Keep a detailed log. Include what was said, what happened, where it happened. Write it in his presence.

    When you're writing the letter demanding the behavior stop, Carnahan suggests including these three parts:

    a. Write a list of the behaviors that occurred. "On this day, you did this . . . I consider this sexual harassment."
    b. Explain how you feel as a result of the harassment.
        + You can't concentrate.
        + You are tense and stressed.

- ◆ Your productivity is down.
- ◆ You have trouble sleeping.
3. Ask someone you trust to act as a witness to your documentation. Send the letter to management.
4. If management does not act upon your letter, and the behavior continues, it's time to take legal action against the perpetrator.

Women Supporting Other Women

As an airline pilot, Suzanne was frequently teased about her gender. She spoke in a low husky voice, and when she gave the captain's greeting, she sounded like she was six feet tall. Most criticism came from women as they disembarked, expecting to see a male captain or a tall woman. Instead, they saw a petite blonde. "Look at that lazy stewardess, sitting in the pilot's chair," they said. Even though they heard her voice, they refused to believe a small woman would pilot a jet. When women as a whole began taking strong stands against sexual harassment, Suzanne's relationships with women strengthened. Now she flies for a major airline and is seldom discounted.

For years, Rozelle used her femininity and dressed seductively when she wanted to get a raise, a promotion or a nice assignment from her boss. Before long, Rozelle realized she only got as far as the person she was manipulating allowed her to go. She was overlooked for major promotions. And, she discovered that other women only confided in her when they wanted Rozelle to get something for them. Now she dresses conservatively and she's had to relocate to create a new image. In her new job, she combines what she learned from her seductress role and empowers women to demand respect.

As a master's student, Trae works independently with a university professor on specific assignments. When he put the moves on her, she stood up to him immediately. "Excuse me, what is it about my body that has anything to do with Statistical Analysis?" Trae asked.

During class break, she overhears women talking about the professor in the bathroom. "He did the same thing to me," Trae says. "This guy is a deliberate harasser. We need to stop him." The women collected additional stories from other students and filed complaints with the department head of Human Resources and the Dean of Graduate Studies.

WOMEN UNITED AGAINST SEXUAL HARASSMENT MAKE A STRONGER STAND.
IT ALL BEGINS WITH ONE BRAVE VOICE.

Fast Fact

If someone is deliberately harassing you, you're not the first victim and you won't be the last unless you take action immediately.

Action

If you're being harassed, bond with other women you trust. Talk about the incident, formulate a plan, then practice your lines so that you're prepared to face the harasser.

"My mother never taught me how to stand up for myself," Carnahan says. "But when my daughter was harassed, I asked her to practice her lines 30 times until she felt prepared."

If you feel you're being harassed, repeat these lines until you are prepared for your next confrontation.

- I don't appreciate your remarks. I don't want you to talk to me like that.
- I have the awesome responsibility for my own reactions to the situations in my life.

EMPOWER YOURSELF: TAKE A STAND AGAINST HARASSMENT

Understanding the sexual harasser's limits empowers you to take a strong stand. How would you react to these situations now?

1. You're driving home from work. Traffic on the interstate finally breaks loose and you speed up. A sleek silver Cadillac pulls up beside you and intentionally runs even with you. You speed up. So does the Cadillac. You slow down. The Cadillac slows also. You become anxious, feeling threatened by the car's presence. You look into the next lane and notice the driver is a co-worker. He smiles and waves. What do you do?

   a. Smile weakly in return. Wave sheepishly. How silly of you to think someone would try to harm you.

b. Speak poorly of his ancestry. Speed up, cut him off, then slam on your brakes. Anyone trying to make a fool out of you deserves to lose his front end.

c. Look at him. Don't smile, don't wave. Tomorrow when you see him, say, "I don't think automobiles are an appropriate power tool for the road. If you need my attention, let's talk about it while we're still at work."

2. You're working at a computer when you see a man standing beside you. You look up. Like always, Ray hovers over you. His belt loop is stretched, he's popped another shirt button, but he's so close, you can hardly focus to see his face. What do you do?

a. Scoot your chair back. When he comes closer, scoot back again.

b. Remove your letter opener from your desk drawer and pop the other buttons on his shirt.

c. Say, "Ray, I can't see you, and I feel uncomfortable when you're this close. Please back away from me."

3. Theodore has been the company's CFO since 1950. He is the nicest man, loves his family and jokes around with everyone in the office. When you started as an accountant last year, everyone called him "Uncle Teddy" because he's such a touchy-feely man. He used to give you little hugs, but lately he's been kissing your cheek. Today, when you give him the monthly financial statement, he tries to kiss you on the mouth. "You're not afraid of an old man?" he says when you resist. You

a. Say, "Of course I'm not. I'm just in a bad mood."

b. Tighten the knot on his tie until his face turns blue. Ask him if anyone in his family wants to know how much he spent last year on personal entertainment.

c. Say, "Theodore, I recognize you as an important person in this company and I don't like to be touched like this."

4. Your boyfriend drives you to work and gives you a kiss as you leave the car. Inside the office, Brian, a male co-worker, joins you as you're walking to your desk. He says, "Long night, eh? Bet you're one hell of a pussycat." You say, "My private life is

none of your business, Brian." Brian says, "Ooooh! Guess who didn't get much sleep." What do you do?

a. Laugh gingerly. Tell yourself Brian's trying to be friendly. Besides, he's a man and can open doors for you that you can't open. Try to be nice to him.

b. Slam your purse into his belly. When Brian laughs again, call your boyfriend and say, "Honey, there's this bully at work who's always trying to put his hands on me. Can you make him stop?"

c. Stop and look directly at Brian. Say, "I consider your comments to be sexually harassing and I don't want you to talk to me like that again." When you get back to your desk, write a letter describing Brian's behavior and give him a copy of the letter. Tell him if he harasses you again, you'll send a copy of the letter to his boss.

5. As a continuing education director, you bring guest speakers to the college from all over the country. A male speaker comes highly recommended to you from several sources. You outline your expectations with him before he arrives. During the conference, a student files a sexual harassment report against him. What do you do?

a. Accept the report. File it in your private records. Say to the student, "I know this person very well and this is not consistent with his behavior. Can you tell me what provoked him?"

b. Invite the speaker into your office. Say, "You came to us highly recommended, and I don't know what's going on. Your sexual harassment will not be tolerated on our campus. You'll have to leave."

c. Accept the report. Tell the student you're scheduling a private conference and the three of you will discuss the event which caused her to file. Tell her you plan to take the claim down to Human Resources and you'll ask both the student and speaker to comment and sign an affidavit.

6. You're an interior designer on a two-hour flight to meet with clients in Milwaukee. During the flight, you strike up a conver-

sation with Ryan, a vice-president of marketing. As a matter of fact, his company is relocating and needs a design consultant for their new offices. You meet him in the lobby of your hotel and have dinner in the restaurant. Ryan is an attentive listener. After the meal, he says, "You're a gorgeous woman. I'd like to get to know you better. Why don't we tidy up this contract in your room? I'll have a bottle of brandy sent up and when we're both comfortable, we can agree on the terms of your project." What do you do?

a. Here you are in Milwaukee with an attentive listener. You know how hard it is to find a man who listens these days? Smile coyly. After all, you're sure he'll keep his word.

b. Slap his face. Say, "Do I look like a hooker? You guys are all alike." Pour water down his shirt, catch the first elevator back to your room.

c. Say, "A brandy would be fine, and I'd like to share it with you right here in the restaurant. I can meet with you tomorrow morning at 9:00 A.M. so we can design a contract that meets both our needs."

7. During the last two to three months, you've been dieting. Sometimes the pounds come off easily. Sometimes they don't. You come into the coffee lounge and face a plate of chocolate-and-caramel-swirled brownies. Adam is also there. Ever since you started the diet, he repeatedly comments on your state of thinness. He sees you drool over the plate and says, "If you eat that stuff, you'll get fat and sassy. Of course, you're already . . . sassy." What do you do?

a. Rush out of the lounge and hide in your office. Call the gym and reactivate your membership. Buy another diet book, swear you'll eat rice for the next year.

b. Say, "Look, Cueball, I guess you're probably not blinding the office with your neon headpiece. Who died and left you prince of weight control?"

c. Say, "Adam, I find your comments offensive. They make both of us feel bad. We have to work together and I don't want rude remarks to get in the way of my productivity. Please don't make comments about my body again."

8. When you joined the company, you found a mentor who helped you move up the corporate ladder. Now you're vice-president of sales, you frequently work overtime, and predominantly with men because there are few women at your level. On your way to the office, you overhear a male junior executive say, "Now that she's this far, I wonder who's left for her to sleep with." What do you do?

   a. Let him sneer. Ignorance runs rampant among youth.

   b. Send a memo to his supervisor. Tell the supervisor you're unhappy with the man's work, you think he might be better suited for another agency. Stay at it until the man comes to his senses or leaves the company.

   c. Step into the young man's office. Say, "I consider your comment about my sleeping arrangements to be sexually harassing. You can get ahead in this office by supporting your co-workers, not by discrediting them. That's how we maintain high productivity here. I want those comments stopped."

9. You're at a sophisticated banquet. Ten people sit around a white linen table while one person tells raunchy jokes filled with four-letter words and trashy sexual scenes. He pauses to pour another glass of wine. What do you do?

   a. Look away from him. Ignore him. He'll get the message.

   b. Grab the wine bottle from him. Say, "I think you've had enough for tonight." When he bellows at you, gag him with your napkin.

   c. Say, "Perhaps those jokes were inappropriate. They were offensive to me. Please don't talk like that in front of me again."

10. You come to work and there's a videotape on your desk. When you play it, you discover it's a tape of several women's body parts, including yours. What do you do?

    a. Rush around the office and confiscate all the copies. Buy new clothes. Change your hair.

b. Stand outside the office and demand to know who filmed the videotape.

c. Take the tape to Human Resources. Include a memo and give details about where you found it, what's on it, and what you'd like Human Resources to do about it. Keep a file of your memo in your office.

GRAND TOTALS

♦ Sexual harassment is not about sex. It's about power.

♦ Your strong self-esteem is the foundation for empowerment.

♦ Your private life is your own business. It does not belong in the workplace. No one has the right to invade your privacy.

♦ You are responsible for your own reactions to the situations in your life.

♦ There are three kinds of harassers: the "unaware," the "deliberate" and the "uncontrollable." Most harassers are unaware. They simply don't know they've offended you.

♦ Education is the best preventive medicine for sexual harassment. Use a positive, commanding tone when setting limits and educating your co-workers.

♦ A deliberate harasser tests your boundaries because your behavior is predictable. Change your behavior and the harasser will leave you alone.

♦ If harassment continues, document the event, send a file to Human Resources, and send a copy to the harasser.

♦ Employers are legally responsible for ending a harassing situation.

♦ Women supporting each other can eliminate sexual harassment from the workplace.

CAPTURING WHAT YOU'VE LEARNED

Things I've learned

_____

_____

Concepts I want to try

_____

_____

Great ideas I want to share with others

_____

_____

Things I want to know more about

_____

_____

INDEX